Four Packs to Freedom

Four Packs to Freedom

Basil Brudenell-Woods

Edited by June Hall

Kangaroo Press

FOUR PACKS TO FREEDOM

First published 1998 by Kangaroo Press
an imprint of Simon & Schuster Australia
20 Barcoo Street, East Roseville NSW 2069 Australia

A Viacom Company
Sydney New York London Toronto Tokyo Singapore

© Basil Brudenell-Woods 1998

ISBN 0 86417 912 X

National Library of Australia
Cataloguing-in-Publication data

Brudenell-Woods, Basil.

Four Packs to Freedom

Includes index.
ISBN 0 86417 912 X
1. Brudenell-Woods, Basil. 2. Australia. Army. Australian Imperial
Force, 2nd (1939-1946) 3. World War 1939-1945 – Prisoners and
prisons – Personal narratives, Australian. 4. Prisoners of war –
Australia – Biography. 5. Escapes – Personal narratives. I. Title

940.5472092

Printed by Australian Print Group, Maryborough, Victoria

Cover illustration by Jeff Lang
based on original by Pam Kenny

Contents

The Resort Walu Beach 30/8/010

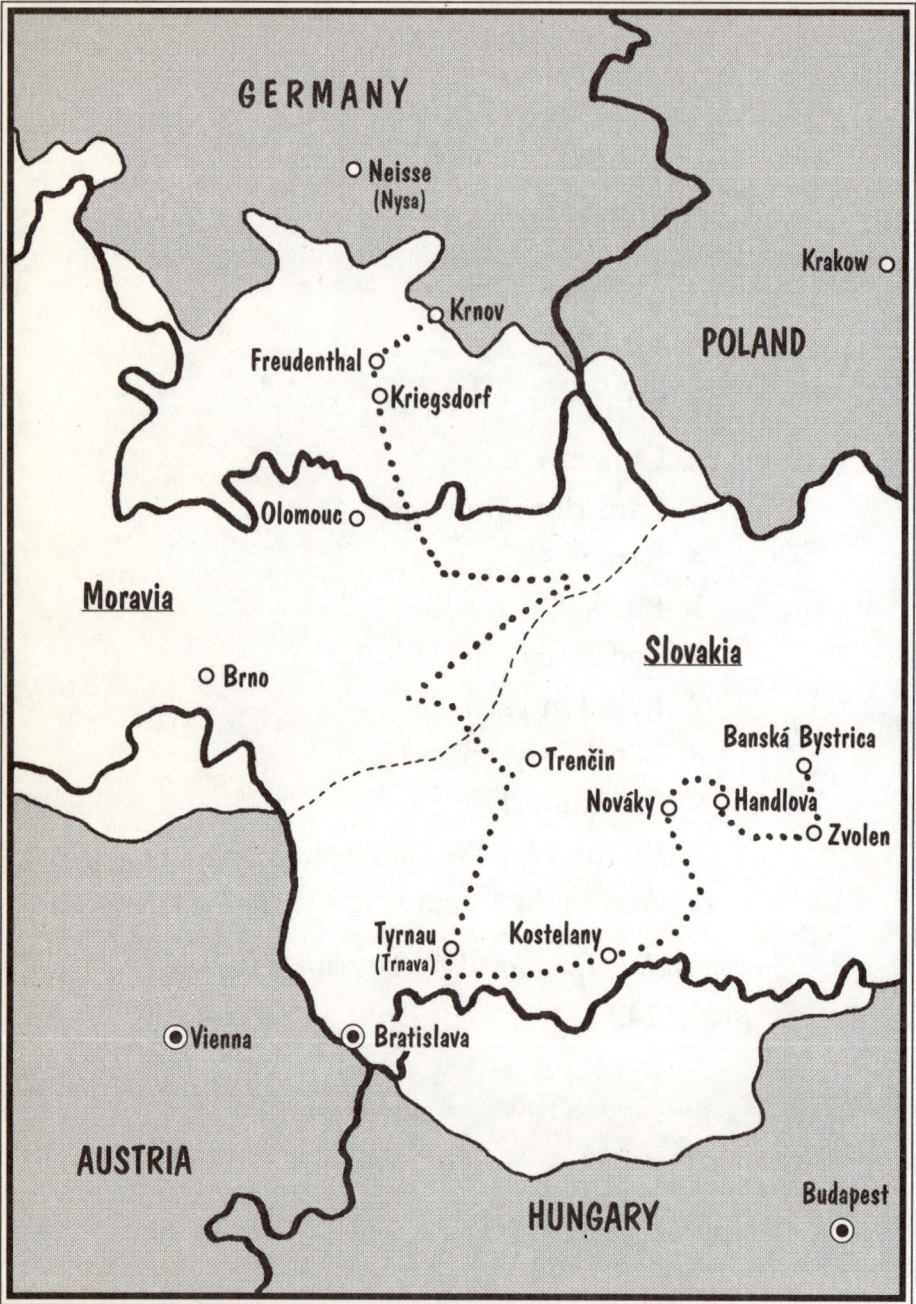

GERMANY

Neisse
(Nysa)

Krakow

Krnov

Freudenthal

Kriegsdorf

POLAND

Olomouc

Moravia

Slovakia

Brno

Banská Bystrica

Trenčin

Nováky   Handlová

Zvolen

Tyrnau
(Trnava)

Kostelany

Vienna

Bratislava

AUSTRIA

HUNGARY

Budapest

National borders established 1938-39

National borders pre-1938

· · · · · · · · · · Approximate escape route

50km

Foreword

Basil Brudenell-Woods, my uncle, enlisted in the Australian Infantry Forces in 1940. He did his basic training at Ingleburn, NSW, sailed in the *Queen Mary* that October, and underwent further training in Palestine. He had been in the North African desert a mere week or ten days when he saw his first and only action. The book begins with his capture by the Germans.

Despite the hardships suffered during three years and three months of internment, this is a tale of incredible good fortune. Basil and his mates had many close shaves while they were on the run in Czechoslovakia, and their final escape to Italy in the midst of one of the most important partisan uprisings of World War II can only be described as miraculous. During the whole of this time, Basil reports, he felt no fear. He was awarded the Military Medal on his return home.

For many years after the war, Basil ran a nursery business with his brother Hereward in Mona Vale, a Sydney seaside suburb. (Bas is still a regular body surfer.) He was interviewed on ABC radio about his escape, the interview was reported in the Sydney press, and *The Australian Women's Weekly* approached him to write his story, but it was not until the early 1980s, in his retirement to a small farm near Taree, that he had the time or inclination to do so.

I found out about the manuscript on a visit to Australia in 1995. With his permission, I edited the text and arranged for a small private printing here in Canada. I also have a more personal connection to this memoir. My mother, Nancie Priestley, Basil's sister, was six months pregnant with me when he was reported missing in action. The family did not find out what had become of him for many months; it was a terrible time in their lives. After the war, however, his escape became the stuff of family legend, though Bas could never be persuaded to discuss what remained for him a painful topic. It has been a wonderful experience to find out, after all these years, what really happened.

June Hall
Halifax, Nova Scotia
Canada
November 1996

Preface

This is a true story, all the events that follow took place, that is, as far as my diary is concerned and my memory will allow. It is a yarn about four men who desired freedom above everything else, and about a wonderful, courageous and fiercely democratic people. I am talking about the people of Czechoslovakia, and in particular about those brave men and women who, at the risk of their own lives, hid us from the Gestapo. Without their help, our freedom would not have been possible.

Many years have passed since the war, but three things have finally inspired me to tell the story of my escape, to have the audacity to write this, my first book.

The first incentive was the greatest. Several years ago, I was cleaning out the top shelf of the wardrobe when I came across the old suitcase I'd brought back from the Middle East in 1944. Inside was the little black diary in which I recorded our experiences during the three months of our escape. Nowhere in those pages, however, will you find any mention of the times when we were concealed by our Czech and Slovak friends, for should the diary have fallen into enemy hands, our friends would have been shot by the Gestapo, and their homes burnt.

Well, I guess most of us, at one time or another, have had the urge to write a book, and then and there I decided not to throw the diary back into the case.

The second spur came in the form of a lonely figure standing by the side of the Pacific Highway near Taree. He had his arm fully extended, with the thumb pointing north, like hundreds of others in recent years, all going in search of work, mainly to Queensland, a state of almost perpetual sunshine and no winter. On his back was the usual large knapsack, containing all his immediate and maybe worldly belongings, plus the ever-necessary sleeping bag. During the brief moments my car approached the figure ahead, many thoughts flashed through my mind — muggings, robbery and even murder — but then I thought of my own daughter, who had recently hitched round Australia and New Zealand, and decided, why not?

I stopped the car, and he thanked me profusely. He sounded like a new arrival in Australia, so I asked him where he came from, and his reply, 'Czechoslovakia', brought back a flood of war-time memories.

He said he was going 'to the end of the road', which amused me greatly. I told him the road went thousands of miles, almost to the top of Australia, and his 'no matter, the further the better' had the familiar ring of a person consumed by wanderlust. In the course of our short journey, he explained that he had become fed up with the drastic, repressive measures of the communist government and had fled his country to find a better way of life. Since leaving Czechoslovakia, he had worked as a lumberjack in Canada, picked apples in New Zealand, and was now looking for work in Australia. He politely refused my offer of a home-cooked meal, and I dropped him a few miles beyond my own destination, as nostalgic memories brought to mind those wonderful people who had befriended us in our hour of need.

The third thing that influenced me to write this book was the quaint saying of a dear old lady. 'Aunty Jane', as she is known to most of the older generation and quite a few of their children, has a heart of gold and gains deep satisfaction from giving, rather than receiving. I came to know Aunty Jane fairly well when she let me use the vacant block behind her house to grow my vegetables. Every once in a while, when I arrived to tend my plants, I would see Aunty all dressed up. When I asked her if she was going to town, she would say she was going to so and so's funeral, and when I asked how old he or she was, her reply was to my way of thinking absolutely beautiful. 'Oh,' she would say, he or she was 'creepin' up.' Aunty herself was 90 years young.

Together the diary, hitchhiker and those words finally persuaded me to act. I realised that I too was 'creepin' up' and if I got to the top, who knows, over the other side Old Nick might be waiting with a wicked grin on his face, or perhaps those lovely angels would beckon me to a beautiful heaven. Either way, my spirit would be looking up or down to the thin crust that supports we poor mortals, and like the Ancient Mariner, trying beseechingly to get someone to listen to, or read my story, and should you finish the last chapter, you will have the satisfaction of hearing my other self breathe a big sigh of relief.

Basil Brudenell-Woods
Taree, New South Wales
1998

1
Tripoli

The tide of battle had rolled away across the desert towards Tobruk, but it left us behind in the ebb.

All that afternoon the battle had raged on the escarpment overlooking the Benina Aerodrome outside Benghazi. Our Battalion, the 2/13th AIF, supported by howitzers, 25-pounders of the 51st Field Regiment, and the Royal Horse Artillery, had been heavily engaged by vastly superior numbers of German tanks, artillery and motorised infantry under the command of Field Marshal Rommel (the Fox).

Our Colonel, 'Bull' Burrows, had been allotted the task of holding the pass near the old Turkish fort of Er Rejima, and the road that ran from there across the desert to Tobruk. I venture to say that the delaying action fought that afternoon was among the most important in the whole North African campaign. It enabled thousands of British and Australian troops, with their stores and armour, to withdraw by the coast road to the stronghold of Tobruk; they might otherwise have been cut off by Rommel's forces, who were taking the shorter route across the desert. Who knows, he may have gone right on down to the Suez Canal.

Our section in HQ Company, which was on a forward slope to the rear of the main fighting, came under mortar and machine-gun fire, aimed mainly at a British artillery gun a few yards to our right, which was engaging the German tanks as they came up the pass and breasted the escarpment. Towards dusk, the gun was put out of action by mortar fire; the Bren gun I was firing was of little use against the tanks as they came over the ridge. If darkness had come only half an hour earlier, it would have enabled us to get back over the ridge a few hundred yards behind us, but such was not to be. On the fourth of April, 1941, between seven and seven thirty in the evening, our position was overrun and we went 'in the bag'.

Now there's a thing. Although the origin of this phrase eludes me for the moment, *The New Oxford Illustrated Dictionary* defines a bag as a receptacle of flexible material with an opening, usually at the top. How

11

damned funny we prisoners would have looked, trussed up like chooks and tied round the neck, with our heads poking out the top.

That night, the other prisoners and I slept on the ground at the Benina Aerodrome. I remember it well. I had taken out my two false teeth and put them in a little cardboard box in my breast pocket. During the night, while I was squirming around, trying to find a comfortable position and keep warm, the box fell out of my pocket. I awoke to the sound of a crunch as a dirty big boot, belonging to one of the German sentries, trod on my box, and away went my two booful fron' teef for the rest of my 'POW' (prisoner of war) life.

The next day we were put in trucks and taken down a long road. We travelled all day — the road seemed endless. Now, all of us go down many roads in our lifetime. Some of us turn to the right, and some to the left, while others take the road straight ahead. I knew only too well that I was travelling in the wrong direction, and to me it was the saddest and longest road of my life.

We sped westward, and although the English troops sitting in the truck alongside me were singing lustily, I felt utterly dejected and numb with despair, to be leaving everything I cared about in the desert dust — my battalion mates, my hopes, and in a way, a cherished dream that I might be able to play a small part in helping to stop the march of a madman.

We reached Tripoli just on sunset. After jumping down from the trucks, we were assembled in three ranks and marched through an opening in a high wall into a large open area, with the sound of two big solid wooden gates clanging shut behind us.

> Onorare Il Pane,
> Gloria di Campo.
> Festa Della Vita…

For the life of me, I cannot remember the fourth line, or for that matter, whether the spelling of those words, or the sequence of the lines, is correct, but suffice to say they were inscribed on the wall above the entrance to a long, single-storey brick building which was to become the abode (God forbid that I call it a home or resting place) of upwards of a hundred or more POWs over the next nine months. Hazarding a guess, I would say those lines meant:

> In honour of bread,
> The land's most glorious produce,
> Life's sustaining feast…

On the other hand, Italian teachers might throw up their hands in despair at this impromptu translation. I say teachers, because we were given to understand that our abode was once an Italian school.

Did I say nine months? Well, to a lot of women, that means an anxious period of waiting, with some fairly hard labour at the end. For us it was bloody hard labour the whole time we were in this camp — missing, presumed dead, unknown to the outside world of family, the life-saving International Red Cross, or the Geneva Convention.

We were a sad and bedraggled lot that first week. Hundreds of POWs came in from the desert battles of El Agheila, Beda Fomm, Er Rejima and Mechili; others were stragglers caught up in Rommel's swift push to Tobruk. Amongst the men were three generals, a colonel, and quite a few officers, in what became known as the 'Benghazi Handicap'. A large number were now 'in the bag'. Rommel was reaping an abundant harvest on the battlefield; it was to be nearly two years before the tide of war would turn in our favour.

I was among the first batch to leave this temporary abode — or so I thought. We were marched down to the wharves, put on board an old tramp steamer and battened down in the holds. The ship was then taken out into the middle of Tripoli harbour, awaiting transport to Italy.

That night our Air Force boys from Malta, as we assumed their departure point to be, came over and plastered the harbour. What a shindig! Bombs exploding all around us; the ack-ack guns in full blast. We prayed that those blokes up above had somehow managed to find out about our particular ship, although we doubted it at this early stage.

After two nights of this, they lowered me over the side of the ship, half unconscious. Just before going over the side, I heard, in my delirious condition, two very different comments, the first from one of my battalion mates: 'There goes poor old Woodsie, wonder if we will ever see him again?' The second came from a general with a patch over one eye, who walked over and took my hand, saying, 'Keep your chin up lad, you will pull through, and the best of luck to you'. I thanked him and decided in my own mind that I would settle for the general's positive approach.

I was fairly sick for a while. When I regained consciousness, I found myself in a hospital bed, my legs swollen, with cotton wool bandages from my thighs to my ankles; I had rheumatic fever. Luckily, I was cared for by a Scottish nurse, the wife of an Italian officer. Each day she would smuggle in some hard-boiled eggs and honey for me; I guess I owe her a debt of gratitude for her kindness in helping me recover.

Ten days to a fortnight later, I was back at the school in time to learn some of the hard lessons of life. I was fairly weak as I got down from the truck and walked through the front gates of our prison. I wish I had a photo. I was dressed in baggy, blue-grey Italian trousers, old boots topped with puttees, an old Italian jacket somewhat similar to our safari topcoat, and an old grey army cap. What a picture! The remarks from some of the boys standing nearby were very much to the point:

'Well, what have we got here — a bloody Eyetie?' said one of the boys.

'No mate,' said another. 'He's the new cook, and now we'll get nothing but bloody macaroni for breakfast, dinner and tea.'

The Kommandant of our camp was a German, and according to some of the boys, he was also a madman. They told me that while I was in hospital, this maniac had rushed into their barracks one night and fired his Luger pistol into the ceiling, yelling and screaming at them to stop smoking.

'You've got to be kidding,' said I with disbelief.

'No bloody fear, you just watch it mate,' they said.

Well, I was soon to find out. We were all lined up and addressed from a balcony overlooking what was once the children's play area. An interpreter passed on the maniac's message, which was to the effect that this was a labour camp, that we would be here for some time, and that any man attempting to escape would be shot. All the while, this big hunk of a man was yelling and screaming, walking back and forth with his hand on a great big Luger pistol in a holster strapped on his belt. With his large, protruding, starey eyes, he created the very picture of a demon possessed.

'Well,' I said to the men on either side of me, 'we are in for a grand old time'.

'You can be bloody sure of that,' they replied.

* * *

We assembled early each morning after a meal that consisted mainly of macaroni, or lentil and vegetable soup. (We were also issued with a small round loaf each and some cheese, our midday meal.) We were divided into working parties and taken in lorries to the various dumps or down to the wharves to unload ships. The two jobs that interested us most were a 'dump' called Fatma, and the wharves. The former because, if you were smart enough, you could steal food and bring it back to camp; this was risky, for the Germans carried out searches at odd times. The wharves created a lot of interest, and the rivalry to get on that particular working party was quite amusing, but more of that later.

The Fatma dump was situated in the desert some miles outside Tripoli. Built by the Italians in their early colonial days, this 'dump' was a collection of storage sheds with big gates at each corner forming a square, somewhat after the style of the old French Foreign Legion forts.

As the trucks came in laden with stores from the ships in the harbour, we were assigned in groups to the various sheds to unload and stack boxes, some of which were quite bulky and heavy. This was my first working detail since coming out of hospital, and I was still fairly weak. I was about to try to lift a large box from the back of a lorry when two arms reached in ahead of me, and a voice with a decidedly Scottish accent said, 'Och mon, move over and gi'e us a go. Ye look a mite weak for this wee bitte goods,' and turning round I looked into the smiling faces of George Adams and his mate George Dorword.

It's funny how some incidents stick in one's mind. I have not forgotten that action, for I would say that those two Scotsmen, and the help they gave me over the following weeks, enabled me to regain my strength. 'Friends in need and in deed.'

When we first arrived at Fatma, the thing that took my eye was the large number of Arabs the Germans had working for them. Their big flowing robes looked most unsuitable for the job. Eventually, we were to take over from them, and I guess there were two main reasons for this.

First was the Arabs' extraordinary sense of hearing. They could hear our planes coming minutes before we could. They'd be unloading the trucks, when all of a sudden there'd be a great commotion and yelling, and with robes flowing behind them, they would take off for the nearest gate and disappear into the desert. This created something of a panic. The trucks were rushed into the sheds and the square was cleared of personnel, but as the target was generally the airfield or the harbour, we were never bombed.

The second reason for getting rid of them was the flowing robes. The guards told us that the Arabs were never searched after a day's work; what they concealed under those robes was nobody's business. Mind you, we were not averse to pinching the stuff ourselves, but to risk taking it back to camp after the day's work, with that madman in charge, was really chancing the odds.

Our main targets were the cartons of concentrated chocolate meant for Rommel's Afrika Korps. These small slabs of chocolate were very sustaining, and some of us were very nearly shot when we were caught with our hands in the boxes, just like small kids caught with their hands in the candy jar.

Late one afternoon, about a week or so later, we returned from our work at Fatma and at once could sense the hostility in our German guards — no smiles, no friendly nods, not that we got those very often, but you could cut the air with a knife. Immediately we thought, 'Hello, something's up,' and how right we were.

That night we were lying on our bunks in the dark (we never did have any lights, complete blackout every night), some of the boys smoking those foul Italian cigarettes made of almost black tobacco, when suddenly the door to our barracks was thrown open and in rushed our mad Kommandant, waving his big Luger pistol and shouting loudly, 'Rauchen Sie nicht!' (No smoking!)

Thinking of what the boys had told me earlier, I was expecting at any moment that this lunatic would start firing his pistol into the ceiling, but this didn't happen. The boys who were having a last puff before dozing off, doused their fags right smartly.

But that was not the end of it. An hour or two later, in rushed several guards, shouting 'Aufstehen, aufstehen! Sie mussen hinaus gehen' (Get up, get up! Go outside) and by the menacing attitude of their lowered rifles, we knew they were in dead earnest. We did not stop to argue the point.

I'll never forget the scene as we lined up in two long files. It was a bright moonlit night. Up on the platform was the mad Kommandant with his interpreter. As he strode up and down, shouting and waving his big Luger pistol, we could hear the sound of bombs exploding in the harbour as our Air Force boys gave it a plastering. This, of course, had the effect of making the madman rant and rave even more wildly.

We soon learnt the reason for this moonlight drama, but he did not have to shout and rave to inform us about sabotage. We knew damn well that some of us were putting handfuls of sand into cans of petrol, and that a few of the artillery boys who worked on the roads running past the ammunition dumps out in the desert were interfering with the Germans' shells. The long and short of the harangue was that sabotage carried a death penalty and that every tenth man would be shot.

There was dead silence. Needless to say, there was an immediate shuffling in the ranks and a hurried counting along the two lines of men, with some wanting to swap places with his next in line.

We were shouted and screamed at for the best part of an hour. Finally his ranting stopped, and with a last word of warning, he shoved the Luger into the holster on his belt and strode down the steps, out through the front gate, and round to his quarters outside the walls of our prison.

'Bloody hell, that was close,' said a man on my left.

'The old bastard really flipped his lid,' remarked a man in the ranks as we were dismissed and marched back into our barracks.

The tension gone, we relaxed somewhat, and as we flopped on to our bunks in the darkness, some wag yelled out, 'Anyone want a cigarette?' Uproar, as they told him what to do with his fag.

*　　*　　*

The harbour: never did I participate in a more delightful way of hindering the enemy's war effort. We were taken down to the wharves to unload the boats, and to our complete surprise and joy, in the holds of one ship we were confronted with hundreds and hundreds of cases of German beer, the best French wines, and wonderful cherry brandies, all from the best and oldest breweries and vineyards of Germany and France. Our eyes goggled. We could *not* believe what we were seeing. Fancy letting thirsty POWs loose amongst this cargo!

Well, we soon organised ourselves. While some of us carried the cases topside to the waiting lorries on the wharf, others would disappear down the dark, narrow passageways between the vast piles of grog. The guards couldn't watch all of us under these conditions, and we soon had the lids of those cardboard boxes ripped open. What nectar of the gods, the best in Europe.

We took turns in this Bacchanalian orgy; I guess there were very few teetotallers amongst us that day. As it drew to a close we became quite merry, and some of us wondered how we could smuggle this delicious beverage back to camp. Well muggins me with the big baggy Italian trousers was chosen as the grog carrier. I tied a thin cord round the necks of some very old bottles of vintage wines and slung them under my trousers, on the insides of my thighs, with the cord suspended from round my neck. I had to move fairly slowly, otherwise they might have done some damage!

*　　*　　*

Many were the plans for escape. Our prison was located alongside a small beach, and sometimes during the summer the big heavy doors in the brick wall of our barracks were thrown open and we were allowed a dip, duly attended by the guards. The idea was that if we could break out at night and swim round the harbour and find a small boat, we could make our way back to Tobruk. But at that time, so early in the fighting, the place was absolutely crawling with German and Italian soldiers and, as we found out later, the Germans had mounted machine guns at either end of the beach, which was briefly lit up by searchlights at different intervals during the night.

The other avenues of escape were the dumps out in the desert where we were making roads and where, as I mentioned before, some of the artillery boys were doing a bit of sabotage. The idea was to jump from the trucks on the way back to camp after work.

I had made friends with a big chap from our battalion named Dave Bray, who had been picked up by some Germans while making his way across the desert to Tobruk with some of his mates after the battle of Er Rejima. They'd unfortunately halted some British trucks on a track in the desert, not realising that the Germans had captured the trucks until they were confronted by a German officer, who appeared from behind one of the halted lorries with a revolver in his hand.

'For you the war is over,' said the officer in polite English.

One day, Dave and I decided that we would try to jump from a truck on the way back from the desert. We put together our water bottles, which we took with us each day, and as much food as possible. The trucks usually went fairly fast, but on this particular day, it was as though the German driver had got wind of our escape plans, for he put his foot down and drove like a bat out of hell. We knew that if we jumped off the lorry, it would mean either a broken arm or leg.

As it turned out, we heard that the loyalty of Arabs from the coastal regions would change according to which side was winning, and that the Germans had offered a reward to any Arab bringing in an escaped prisoner — the rumour was dead or alive. We guessed that our chances of being brought back alive were fairly slim, and with 500 miles of desert to cross, survival would be unlikely.

*　　*　　*

Let me tell you a little story about one of the great characters of our camp. Ted Broomhead was a minister of the church from Adelaide, either Presbyterian or Methodist — I forget which, but what does it matter? Sure, most of us had our faith, but under the conditions of POW life the universal religion of the teachings of the Lord — to love and help your fellow man — was of paramount importance, and Ted had those qualities to the nth degree. No, he wasn't a preacher in that sense of the word, but boy, could he tell a story.

After tea at night, while we were lying on our bunks, Ted would stroll up and down the passageways telling us stories, a chapter each night. One story in particular stood out; it enthralled us all. Now Ted was not very tall, but what he lacked in height he made up in stature. He was terrific, in the sense that he kept us spellbound, and during the telling of these yarns, our minds and thoughts were quite oblivious to our sordid surroundings. What was so amazing was the fact that during all the time he was relating the story, not once did he refer to a book. What a colossal memory.

But I digress from the little tale I was going to tell you about Ted. One Sunday afternoon, who should come stamping in through the main gates but the mad Kommandant. We thought, 'Hello here's trouble,' but to our surprise, he walked up to Ted and said, 'Kommen Sie mit' (Come with me). Now Ted, who could speak a bit of German (and he was not one to argue), decided to accompany the Kommandant and together they marched out through the main gates.

Well, we all speculated, and it being Sunday, some of us thought 'Old Starey Eyes' wanted to repent, and would ask Ted to give him his blessing. Others, with not so lofty ideals, thought that would be the day. Anyway, late in the afternoon, just before tea, Ted returned to camp with quite an unsteady gait, his hat at a decidedly cock-eyed angle and a bleary look in his eyes.

We crowded round, and from what we could make out from Ted's mumbling speech, 'Old Starey Eyes' wanted nothing more than a drinking companion. Ted was taken round to the German canteen, where the Kommandant pulled his Luger pistol from its holster, and placing it on the bar counter, said in a loud, truculent voice, 'Trinken' (Drink), and motioned to the soldier behind the bar, who quickly poured two large glasses of beer. As I said before, Ted was not one to argue, and swallowing the contents, held up his hands with a gesture to indicate that he had had enough. Not so with 'Old Starey Eyes'. Lifting up his Luger and slamming it down on the counter, he shouted 'Trinken,' as the barman poured two more glasses. So it went the whole afternoon, with the madman yelling and screaming at Ted, telling him how Germany would win the war and what a great day it would be when Hitler ruled the world. Before the afternoon grog session had ended, Ted must have consumed half a dozen glasses.

That night our Air Force boys really gave the harbour and surrounds a hammering. Outside our gates was a big German anti-aircraft gun, which to us was ear-shattering, and we hoped and prayed the RAF knew the location of our camp. Well how they missed us I'll never know; we could actually hear one bomb whistling down a second or two before it exploded, putting the ack-ack gun and crew out of action and blowing open our front gates.

All this time our mad Kommandant had the guards outside the walls marching up and down, and he was yelling and screeching 'Singen, singen' to them. Their marching songs rose in crescendo as the sound of the bombs died away, but when the shrill whistling sound of more falling bombs could be heard, their voices faded away to a murmur, to be followed by another outburst of shouting from the Kommandant, 'Singen, singen,' and as the sound of their voices rose heavenwards, I guess it was accompanied by their prayers. While this circus was going on outside the walls, we inside, although fearing the worst, were laughing our heads off and quite enjoying the performance.

*   *   *

The weeks and months dragged on and it seemed a natural thing, just as in any big concern or work place back in civvy street, that you teamed up with one or two others for companionship. As I mentioned before, my particular mate was Dave Bray, who came from the northern rivers of New South Wales and had a banana plantation on the Tweed River just outside Murwillumbah. His father was one of the earlier settlers on the river and had the No. 1 post box for the area. Dave and I and a few other Aussies became great friends and a wonderful moral support for each other in our periods of depression.

At night, lying on our bunks, the yarns would begin to flow. One night everyone was wound up and eventually the boys were clamouring for Woodsie to tell them a story.

'Well,' I said, 'this is a true story, believe it or not'.

There was a hoot of derisive laughter and a voice came out of the darkness. 'Cut out the bullshit, Basil, and get on with the yarn.'

'This story is no bullshit,' I said. 'It actually happened back in Palestine, at Kilo 89, in our battalion lines. We had just come in from a fairly tough route march in the desert, and the boys were given time to go to the toilets and smarten up a bit before falling in for a full company parade and company commander's inspection. We were all lined up when it was noticed that there was one man missing from the battalion area guard.'

'Don't tell us, I'll bet he was down at the shithouse with Gyppo tummy,' said a voice out of the darkness.

'No bloody fear,' I said. 'He was in his tent when a company orderly arrived to inform the corporal of the guard that the missing soldier was to fall out at once, dressed as he was.

20

'Now if you knew Blue Thompson as we knew him (he had red hair, of course, and got into more strife than Ned Kelly), you would understand what followed. I don't know whether he was going to the showers, or just changing his clothes, but he was in his birthday suit. Blue was always one to take advantage of a difficult situation, so when the corporal insisted that he fall out immediately, Blue grabbed his rifle, pulled on his boots, put on his webbing, slapped his hat on his head and marched out on parade.

'The corporal's eyes bulged and the loud voice of the company s'gt major rang out: 'Corporal, get that man properly dressed."

Well, the boys really liked the story. There were a lot of rude remarks about Blue and the obvious question came out of the darkness, 'What the bloody hell happened to Blue?'

'Well,' I said, 'Blue was paraded before the company officer in charge, who got to the point right smartly.

"Private Thompson, how do you intend to explain your disorderly conduct?' said the OC with a steely look in his eye and a touch of sarcasm in his voice.

'Blue maintained that he was only carrying out the corporal's orders, as any good soldier would.

'The OC looked at Blue and said, 'Private Thompson, I'm giving you a week's pack drill and consider yourself lucky,' and Blue was marched out under escort.

'Now, if you know anything about pack drill, it's a fairly hard business. The participant is marched up and down the parade ground hour after hour, fully clothed (especially Blue), with full equipment (pack, rifle and webbing), with a break of ten minutes on the hour to allow the soldier to rest in his tent. Blue told me afterwards that he had never drunk so much beer in his life, for during those breaks, the boys smuggled in enough grog for half a dozen men, let alone one.'

*　　　*　　　*

The nine months of our isolation drew to a close. One morning, with a lot of yelling and shouting, we were assembled with all our packs and marched down to the wharves, where we boarded what looked like a tramp steamer. Once outside the harbour, instead of being battened down below for the whole voyage, we were allowed up on deck, the reason being (or so we thought) that one of our own submarines might sink the ship by mistake as it crossed the 'Med,' not knowing we were on board. I had heard, probably by latrine news, that a POW ship had been sunk somewhere near Greece with the loss of quite a few lives.

It took over two days to reach Italy, as we hugged the coast most of the time, with the shores of Africa on our port side. Boy, was it cold! And what a motley crew we POWs were, unshaven and bleary-eyed, with our coats wrapped around us. Most of us spent nearly the whole voyage huddled on deck, and I suspect that in the boys' minds was the thought of those submarines lurking in the depths below. To prove the point, close inshore we saw several sunken ships with their masts sticking out of the water. Finally we slipped across the strait between Tunisia and Sicily, with the island of Pantelleria off to starboard, and dropped anchor in the harbour at Palermo. From there we were taken by train to a transit camp at Castelvetrano.

What a cold and hungry lot we were as we lay on the straw under a huge canvas tent. We stayed there for about ten days before being shipped across the strait to Taranto, where we spent the night in an underground shelter whilst the harbour was being bombed by our Air Force. The following morning, we boarded a train and once again were on our way to an unknown destination, heading north, maybe right up into Germany. We were a very subdued lot, not much talk, as we slowly made our way up the west coast of Italy. We all realised that for every mile that passed, we were getting farther and farther from our own forces, and that the goal of this journey was not a winning post — indeed, we were losing the match. My mates and I felt pretty miserable, our spirits at a fairly low ebb.

'What are our chances of getting away under these conditions?' I said to my big mate Dave, who was sitting alongside me.

'Bloody well impossible, Basil,' he said, 'especially if they take us right through to Germany. But cheer up, if we do go there, we will get a change of diet — no more macaroni'.

We hugged the shoreline most of the day, occasionally catching glimpses of the Mediterranean, and that night we saw a most amazing and spectacular sight as streams of molten lava poured down the mountainside of Vesuvius. The guards told us that it was many years since that had occurred, so we just hoped that it did not blow its top whilst we were passing, having in mind the catastrophic disaster that engulfed Pompeii in Roman times. So we passed through this land of wonderful antiquities, and mid-afternoon we glimpsed another very interesting sight, as in the distance was the Leaning Tower of Pisa. At last, just on dusk, we arrived at our destination, Chiavari, near Genoa, where we were to stay for well over a year.

2
Chiavari

JANUARY 1942. Campo di prigionia di Guerra, Numero Cinquanta Due, in other words, Prisoner of War Camp Number 52. Well, at long last our abode had a name and a number, and although we were damn glad to leave the heat, lice, labour and sandstorms of North Africa, the damp, freezing cold of a northern Italian winter was no joke, and as it progressed, the cold became very bitter indeed. We were told by the guards that this was the coldest winter for almost thirty years.

By day the ground was a quagmire, but at night it froze so hard that even a pick couldn't penetrate it; in the mornings it was like walking on a skating rink. How does John Denver put it? 'Sometimes a cold wind blows a chill in my bones?' Oh boy, how true that was when the wind blew down from the Alps.

Our living quarters were long wooden huts of one or two storeys, and as in Africa, we slept on two-tiered bunks. My big mate, Dave Bray, who slept on the top bunk above me, was so cold that his shivering shook the whole frame. A remark of mine ('Hey, Dave, can't you stop rocking the flaming boat?') brought the apt reply: 'Basil, this is not brass monkey weather, but a full-grown gorilla's.' There were a lot like Dave, big men, who nearly froze to death on the meagre rations of macaroni, thin watery vegetable soup, and one small round loaf of bread a day between two men. However, the human species is very tenacious, and we survived.

Although we didn't know it at the time, we were to be in this camp for well over a year, and we settled into a routine. Again, each hut was under the charge of one of our sergeants or warrant-officers. There was a hut parade each morning after we'd eaten an early morning snack and tidied up our bunks. The men stood by their beds while our sergeant, Reg Crawley, accompanied by an Italian sergeant who could speak English, checked the names and numbers of all the men.

We were given fold-up envelopes to write our first letters home in many months, with the assurance from our Italian camp commandant that they would reach their destination. How we looked forward to a reply from our families, whom we had not heard from for a long time, and I guess they felt the same way.

To our great relief, it was not long after our arrival that we received our first Red Cross parcels, sent through the International Red Cross in Switzerland. What a godsend! In that intense cold, how we blessed those dedicated workers around the world; their splendid work saved hundreds of prisoners' lives, both physically and mentally.

It was because of that wonderful institution that POW camps in Europe were saved from becoming places of humanity lost and degraded in mind and body such as existed in the Gulag Archipelago in Siberia and the Nazi concentration camps. Instead they were fairly well-organised seats of learning. If one so desired, one could attend classes in almost any subject, for amongst us were men from all walks of life, including university professors and teachers of almost anything you might wish to learn. I might add that without this occupational therapy, I'm sure a lot of men would have gone round the bend. High praise for those teachers!

It was through the Red Cross in Switzerland, you see, that we obtained study books, writing materials, musical instruments and, to our complete surprise and joy, a piano, for one of our fellow POWs was a brilliant Australian pianist. He played some wonderful tunes at the camp concerts, a great boost to camp morale.

In a few of the plays, some of the actors dressed as women. Their performance was so excellent that quite a few of the boys got really randy and followed them back to their quarters after the show, not that anything untoward happened. However, after a couple of plays with female impersonators, the Allied officer in charge of maintaining order amongst the POWs called a parade, and our padre gave us a lecture on women-hungry men amongst men.

The desire for freedom was uppermost in our minds at all times, and an escape committee was organised by 'Tiny' Cameron — he was over six feet tall — a fighter pilot who had been shot down over the North African desert. What a wonderful character he was, cheerful at all times and a great inspiration to all and sundry who came in contact with him. He was not averse to having his little joke, and the following story makes a fascinating yarn, though I heard it only at second hand, so cannot vouch for its authenticity.

As the story goes, Tiny put on a midnight supper and invited some of his immediate friends, who of course expected a good feed from the Red Cross parcels. When their dixies were filled with delicious meat, the men couldn't believe their eyes, and plied Tiny with questions as to its origin.

Tiny kept silent during the meal, which all enjoyed with mouth-watering gusto, and come the end of the feast, their host announced that they had just eaten the camp commandant's dog. There was deadly silence, then a concerted rush for the door, and quite a noise outside as the boys were sick. So much for the old saying, 'It's only mind over matter'.

Anyway, all jokes aside, to get back to the serious business of escape, this likeable bloke had organised a tunnel dig under one of the huts, hoping to emerge on the outside of the barbed wire. The soil from the tunnel was to be spread under the other huts. Well, one night, as we were keeping watch out the hut window, the perimeter searchlight suddenly shone down between the huts, and in its beam we could see big Tiny and his co-worker standing stock still, holding a large sack of soil between them.

Well, that was the end of the beginning of that tunnel. The next morning, into the camp came the camp commandant, followed by a number of guards, and after a detailed search the tunnel was found. A lot of restrictions followed.

*   *   *

How we looked forward to the coming of spring, particularly after our first grim winter. As the trees on the hills surrounding the valley burst into life, we knew that the summer could not be far behind.

The frugality of the area's good farmers was brought to our notice each morning, when we could see the womenfolk leaving the nearby village with rakes over their shoulders, and carrying large pieces of hessian. The women would proceed to walk slowly up the nearby hillsides, raking up all the dead leaves that had fallen from the trees during the preceding winter. When they'd finished raking the leaves into big piles, they would gather them onto the hessian pieces and carry them down to farms on the valley floor, where the leaves would be spread over the fields and either ploughed or dug in to act as humus in place of fertiliser.

The old colonel in charge of the camp was the exact opposite of that madman in North Africa. He was a kindly old soul, and occasionally of a Sunday would let a few of us go for a walk up the valley, accompanied by the guards. It was during those walks that I couldn't help noticing the industrious methods of the Italian farmers; there was not a square foot of ground that was not being used. In between the rows of grapevines they grew wheat, and between the vines themselves they grew cabbages, cauliflowers and other vegetables.

We heard that their thrift was duly rewarded by Hitler, who sent trainloads of coal down through the Brenner Pass into Italy in exchange for surplus and not-so-surplus grain and other foodstuffs. The old saying, 'Fair exchange is no robbery', did not quite apply, as Hitler had his own quotation, 'All's fair in love and war'.

*   *   *

The warmer weather was with us now, and for us Australians, who were not accustomed to the very cold European winters, it was like manna from heaven. On hot summer days, the boys all wore shorts, ranging from old cut-down trousers to underpants. The long summer twilight was something new to us, and to sit out on the steps until about nine o'clock in the evening, listening to the beautiful dulcet tones of the nightingales down by the Lavagna River nearby, was a panacea to our confined existence.

The Red Cross parcels were arriving regularly now. They were stacked on arrival in the big hut inside the camp and opened for inspection by the camp commandant before being apportioned amongst the various huts. Now to see the looks on the faces of the commandant and the guards standing nearby, as the parcels were opened, was rather pathetic, for we knew that most of the articles in the parcels were unobtainable in Italy. Most probably their propaganda ministry had broadcast that the Allies were starving, yet here before their very eyes, they were seeing such things as tinned oatmeal, tea, plain round Canadian biscuits, Australian raisins, and quite a few other goodies, being sufficient in calories and vitamins, together with the Italian rations, to keep one alive. Although it was never intended as such by the International Red Cross, those parcels were a favourable reminder to the Germans and Italians that the Allies were not starving.

Northern Italy in the summer can be really hot. This summer was no exception, and some of the boys were in the habit of sleeping in the nuddy. Now the general rule was that those boys sleeping on the top bunks kept their Red Cross parcels on the floor under the bottom bunks.

It must have been well after midnight on this particular occasion. There was a hell of a noise on the bunk next to Dave's and mine, and we were awakened by the sound of yelling as the bloke on the top bunk shouted, 'You bloody bastard, pinching my food. I'll knock your bloody block off'. And with that he took a flying leap from his bunk, landing almost on top of the bloke who was kneeling down ratting his parcel. Well, the bloke took off like a startled hare, with his pursuer screaming dire threats, and out the door they flew. What took our fancy was the fact that neither had a stitch on.

Outside it was bright moonlight. The Italian guards doing night patrol outside the wire couldn't believe their eyes as the two raced madly round and round between the huts, and their usual form of address, 'Georgio, Georgio' (after King George V), rang out in the night air. I'll bet they'd never seen anything like it before; they must have thought, 'How randy can you get!'

It was on one of those twilight evenings, while Dave and I were sitting outside on the steps of our hut, that we were approached by a tall, wiry-looking Australian who also lived in our hut. We had heard his name at roll call, but as he slept on the top floor, we did not know him very well. Little did we know that this tough-looking Aussie was to play a most important part in our dash for freedom.

'My name's Bill Irvine,' he said. 'Do you mind if I join you blokes?' He settled himself down on the steps, and after a bit of small talk, got around to telling us how he became a POW.

He was a 6th Divvy bloke and had been in all the battles in the first push up the desert against the Italians. From there his battalion, the 2nd/4th, was shipped across to Greece to try to halt the German advance into that country, but to no avail, for they had to withdraw against vastly overwhelming German armour and infantry, all the while being bombed and strafed by the Luftwaffe. Finally they were evacuated.

He was on the RN destroyer *Hereward* when German stukas dive-bombed and sunk the ship. He and many others remained in the water, desperately clinging to bits of flotsam, for upwards of eight hours or more before they were picked up by enemy motor torpedo boats from the mainland and taken into captivity.

Bill had a dry sense of humour, but he was one of those quiet blokes who are not given to saying very much, and we had to ply him with questions to obtain all this information. He came from Victoria, where he and his brother had a farm, and he was, I guess, like a lot of the men who till the soil from daylight to dark on their own. They acquire a kind of quiet reserve, and although not given to much conversation, they are staunch and dependable.

We three became great mates and used to exchange various articles from our Red Cross parcels, according to our likes and dislikes. What we always appreciated were the small packets of tea included in most of the parcels.

I must mention a wizard of an idea that some brain thought up while we were in this camp. The strange little contraption, which we used to make a hot brew of tea, was a wonderful boost to the morale of the boys.

Let me explain how it was made, and how it worked.

The base could be any old piece of wood, mostly scrounged from odd pieces of timber lying around. Quite a few were made from the slats of timber under the boys' bunks, generally about 18 inches long by 4 inches wide. Attached to the base by old nails, which we found lying under the huts or took from the walls where they would not be missed, was our little fire machine, as we used to call it. The machine was made out of empty food tins (from our Red Cross parcels), which we first flattened.

The whole thing was like a miniature blacksmith's forge, but instead of bellows, at one end were bits of tin shaped into a propeller. The propeller was attached to a miniature windlass handle, which in turn was attached to and enclosed within the framework of the machine. When the handle was turned, it rotated the propeller blades, drawing in air on the open side and forcing it along a little tunnel, at the end of which the air went up and out through small holes in the bottom of a tin sitting on top of the framework. In the tin we put anything that would burn — bits of old cardboard, chips, or pieces of stick. We would perch our little billy can on top of this tin, set alight the chips or sticks, turn the handle furiously, and it was only a matter of a few minutes before the water boiled.

Try to visualise the scene, as just on dusk, there would be hundreds of men squatting round these little fire machines. The picture resembled an Arab encampment, with smoke swirling around and above the crouching figures, so intent on their precious brew. To think that those precious little black leaves, probably picked from the bushes of a tea plantation on the hillsides of far-off Assam, in India, could bring so much pleasure and enjoyment to so many men under the duress of POW life.

*   *   *

In the camp, we had a hut full of sailors who had been picked up after their ships had been sunk in the Mediterranean. One morning, Dave, who had been for a walk round the camp, came racing into the hut shouting, 'Come and have a look boys, something's going on at the sailors' hut'.

Well we all left what we were doing and hurried outside. There was quite a commotion. The old colonel was there with a full guard, and the sailors were lined up in two ranks outside their hut. He beckoned to a couple of his guards and went inside, and it wasn't very long before he came out, his face a deep puce colour, a picture to behold. Then walking up and down before the sailors, he harangued them for nearly half an hour.

You know, we used to wonder how those sailors came by their never-ending supply of wood. Well, we were left in doubt no longer, for when the colonel had given orders for the sailors to pack their gear, and we had seen the last of them marching out the gate, singing, on their way to another plot of land reserved for we by-products of war, we all trooped into their hut to see what had caused their sudden departure.

Those sailors had done a grand job whittling away at the posts that stood in line down the middle of the hut, supporting the roof. They had also gone to work on their bunks. It was amazing how skilfully they had pared the wood away without the Italians noticing their artistry, the problem being of course that the diameter of the posts was well on the way to letting the huts collapse round the sailors' ears.

'Gawd struth chum,' said a young English chap alongside me. 'The cunning bastards! Why didn't I think of that?'

*   *   *

And so the days and months passed until, in the first two weeks of September, rumours began to filter into the camp. As usual, the best place to get any news was the dunny, a long building down at the northern end of the camp. It was quite a sight to see the boys squatting down in a row over an open concrete drain attending to their morning toilet, with the water sluicing away underneath them. It reminded me of crows sitting on a stockyard fence back home in the bush.

'Have you heard the latest rumour?' said a bloke squatting alongside me.

'No,' I said, 'but I know the camp's bulldust seems to float around this place fairly thickly'.

'They say that Italy has capitulated, and that King Victor Emmanuel has accepted Mussolini's resignation.'

'Fair dinkum,' I said. 'Where did you get that bit of news?'

'It's supposed to be true. One of our sergeants was talking to an Italian guard at the gate. This Eyetie has a fair smattering of English, and he told the sergeant that on July 25th there was a meeting of the Grand Council in Rome, which voted in favour of the King having supreme power in Italy, and that Marshall Badoglio was made Premier and was in control of the armed forces.'

Just for a moment there was a dead silence, then a babble of voices as this amazing bit of news began to sink in, and some of us were already thinking of those front gates being thrown open to give us our freedom.

'What happens next?' I said. 'Does this mean that Italy has thrown in her lot with the Allies?'

'Hold hard, don't rush your fences,' said one of the brains of the camp. He was an English and history teacher back home in Australia, and had just arrived on the scene to attend to Mother Nature.

'You blokes want to realise,' he said, 'that there are a mighty lot of Germans in this country, and don't forget Mussolini's black-shirt fascists. I don't want to dishearten you blokes, but do you think for one moment that Hitler is going to leave the underbelly of Europe wide open for the Allies to just walk in and attack his forces thousands of miles closer to his homeland?'

This piece of studied reasoning had a somewhat sobering effect on the boys and brought their minds and thoughts right back to 'Parliament House'.

Excitement in the camp was at fever pitch. Every man jack of us collected all the food from our Red Cross parcels and what personal belongings we could carry, tying them up in a neat bundle in our coats or jumpers. Bill, Dave and I had decided to stick together and try and make our way over the Alps into the haven of Switzerland, and I guess most of the boys in the camp had the same idea.

*   *   *

23 SEPTEMBER 1943: a day we were all to remember. There was great activity over at the guard house and a lot of comings and goings, and we in the camp knew that this was the time, if ever, to try and make a break for freedom. The Italian guards, however, were still patrolling the outside perimeter of the camp and manning the machine-guns up in the watch-towers.

A big crowd of us gathered at the main gate and all along the barbed wire which enclosed the camp. It was the old story of 'being on the inside and looking out,' and even though we yelled at them to open the gates, the guards took no notice of us, keeping their rifles levelled in our direction. The language and curses that flew across the wire from we boys to those Italian guards would have made the air blue, but our efforts were all to no avail. It seemed that this was not to be our day.

Towards midday, as we milled around the front gate of our camp, we looked over towards the main road, which was on the other side of the river, and saw truck-loads of heavily armed German soldiers pulling up. The men jumped down and started running across the narrow bridge spanning the river, making towards our camp.

With anger and despair we shouted at the guards, but it was a forlorn hope. Our efforts were all in vain. Soon our prison guards were replaced by German soldiers, and the departing Italians were followed by our curses and language that would make your hair curl.

The German replacements were battle-hardened troops. We knew that they would be more alert than the Italians, and even though we were desperate men, common sense prevailed. We all realised that our chances of making a break through the wire that night were fairly slim, and to prove the point, the Germans let off bursts of machine-gun fire at odd intervals during the night. We were a very dejected lot, and you could see the looks of disappointment written on the boys' faces as they sat around on their bunks that evening.

'I reckon we'll be going north, maybe tomorrow,' said Dave.

'You're bloody cheerful, but I think you may be right,' said Bill. I was silent for a while, still feeling frustrated and angry that those guards had not opened the gates of our camp.

'Well, you blokes,' I said, 'Germany is a long way off. Maybe we can jump from the train before we get there.' This remark seemed to raise their spirits a little, and the reply — 'We'll give it a bloody good go, Basil' — bore out the feelings of all the men standing round.

We only remained in the camp for a few more days, but during this time I saw something that was almost unbelievable in this day and age.

When the Italians threw in the sponge, Hitler, of course, poured large numbers of reinforcements into Italy. The main road south, running down the coast near Genoa, ran past our camp on the other side of the river. The scene we witnessed during the next few days was reminiscent of the old days of the American Wild West, for hundreds of horse-drawn covered wagons went by on that road hour after hour taking supplies (I assume) down the boot of Italy to the forward troops. It was an amazing sight that still lingers in my memory.

About five days later there was a lot of shouting at the guard house outside the main gate, and soon after, a German officer came out accompanied by several non-commissioned officers (NCOs) and some of the guards. Making their way to the main gate, they entered the camp and approached the British officer who was in charge of all the POWs. We knew what was on the cards, and it wasn't too long before our hut leader, Sergeant Reg Crawley, entered our barracks accompanied by a German NCO. We didn't have to guess what was coming next.

'Well boys, this looks like it,' said Reg. 'Get all your things together. We are moving camp.'

The whole camp was to be evacuated. We were assembled outside our huts with our belongings and marched out through the main gate, closely guarded by German soldiers on either side and to the front and rear of the long column as we slowly made our way down to the railway siding at Chiavari. Awaiting us was a long line of cattle trucks, and as we threw our bundles into the trucks and clambered up after them, we did not have to guess our destination.

It had to be Germany. Our hearts sank as we realised that we were being taken into the heart of Europe, far away from our own forces (little did we know how far), and there and then, Bill, Dave and I decided that if it was humanly possible, we were going to try to jump off that train and make our way to Switzerland.

How many men to each truck? Well I don't exactly remember, but I do know that back home it was generally the case to put 11 or 12 horses or 14 cattle in each truck. With us it was quite a different matter. They shoved us in those trucks until there was barely room to move, and as I said before, I don't remember the exact number, but it was probably between 20 and 30.

'Why don't they pour in some bloody sardine oil?' said some wag.

We had filled our water bottles at the camp, which was just as well as it turned out, and before the big solid doors of our trucks were slid shut and bolted from the outside, small loaves of bread were passed into each truck, one to each man, and there was also a can about the size of a kerosene tin in which to relieve ourselves.

All that day we sped across the Lombardy Plains, our morale at a low ebb, especially with the suffocating heat of the grim, overcrowded cattle trucks. We took it in turns to stand at two small, iron-barred windows, taking in gulps of fresh air.

Well, try as we may, we could not prise up the heavy floor planks or loosen the strong walls of our truck, mainly because we had no suitable tools to work with, only our bare hands. A few men in some of the other trucks were lucky enough to find some loose planks and managed to jump from the train. Some were killed in the attempt.

One of our battalion mates, a Lieutenant Harold Peterson, was one of those who escaped. After spending some months with the partisans, he managed to cross the Swiss Alps to freedom — a great effort. Other boys who managed to escape were working on farms at the time of the Italian decision to throw in their lot with the Allies. Amongst them was another soldier from our battalion, one Bob Murray, who was with the Italian partisans for 20 months and was promoted to lieutenant by the British Command.

What a tale I heard from Bob. I suspect that he must be the only

Australian who witnessed the execution of Mussolini and his mistress. Bob was with a large band of partisans who ambushed and surrounded their cars (which were packed with notes and coins of different currencies) as Mussolini and his party tried to escape into Switzerland — they were only four hours from the Swiss border. Bob told me that when Mussolini was shot, he showed no fear and held up his arm in the Fascist salute, whereas his mistress screamed and yelled in abject terror.

'Where the hell do you think they are taking us?' asked Dave.

'Don't you know?' was Bill's dry comment. 'We are on the grand tour of Europe, staying at the best hotels.' Bill did not speak very often, but when he did his remarks generally suited the occasion.

After crossing the Lombardy Plains, our first stop was Verona, where we arrived late in the afternoon at a big depot or marshalling yards that served as the departure point for trains going up through the Brenner Pass into Austria.

This time their freight was of the human kind. Pulled up on the various tracks around us were trainloads of Yugoslav partisan prisoners, and Italian soldiers who had been let down to relieve themselves. It did not take us long to realise that the Italians were also prisoners, or at least under strict supervision, for the German guards ordered them back into the trucks, and when they were slow to obey orders, revolvers were used to enforce the commands. I saw one Italian who was shot in the leg and then dragged up inside the truck by his fellow men. These guards meant business, and we knew that at each end of our train they had mounted machine-guns and searchlights.

After leaving Verona, we made our way northwards up the Largarina Valley until we came to a small railway station named Ala, where the train stopped. We could hear a lot of shouting and what sounded like orders being given on the platform outside. Suddenly there was the sound of bolts being drawn, and our door slid open to reveal two guards with a large container of water. What a great relief this was, as most of the men had drunk nearly all the water in their water bottles whilst crossing the hot Lombardy Plains, and we were starting to show the first signs of dehydration.

A sad thing happened at Ala. About 4 o'clock in the afternoon — I have the time, place and event in my diary — a few of us poked our heads out the door to see what was going on. We could see guards dishing out water to the men in other trucks along the whole length of the train. Meanwhile, two or three German officers were walking back and forth along the platform with their revolvers drawn, shouting 'Schnell, schnell' (quickly, quickly) and gesticulating to the boys to pull their heads back into the trucks. Well, some of the boys were a bit slow in obeying orders, so one of the German officers raised his revolver and fired into the truck next door, killing poor Charley Perry, a quiet unassuming sergeant in a Victorian battalion.

There were howls of rage from the boys as they yelled at the officer, telling him in lurid language what he had done. The grim-faced man strode over to the truck, and levelling his revolver at the boys, told them, in halting English, to be quiet, then ordered two of the guards to carry Charley's body out of the truck and lay it on the platform. Sadly, I suppose, Charley's relatives would have been told eventually of his burial in some obscure cemetery in northern Italy.

We passed Bolzano and chugged our way slowly up through the Brenner Pass, mountains towering above us on either side. How small and insignificant they made us feel as we gazed forlornly out through the iron bars. I think I speak for the others as well when I say that our spirits were at a fairly low ebb; a kind of sombre quietness hung over us, with very little conversation amongst the boys as we travelled farther and farther towards an unknown destination.

I think it was about midnight on the second night that we stopped at a small station somewhere in Austria. Our sliding doors were drawn back and we could see by the dim station lights glowing in the darkness that there were girls standing on the platform, which was lined with German soldiers. An officer strode up and down, and speaking good English, told us to remain in the trucks and hand our dixies to the girls, who were dishing out hot soup from the large containers standing on the platform outside each door.

What a wonderful surprise. We handed out our dixies to a lovely girl, who seemed to be in her early twenties, and when she handed me back my dixie, I said 'Gnädiges, Fräulien' (Thank you ever so much lass). She gave me a timid smile and said, 'Bitte schön' (Not at all), and I could see that she had tears in her eyes.

We must have appeared a ragged and sorry sight, with several days' growth of beard, and we probably smelt to high heaven. Taking a quick look to left and right, I could see outstretched arms holding dixies, which were filled by these ministering angels.

Finally, the heavy doors were slammed shut and bolted and the train slowly pulled out into the night, with some of us waving through the iron bars, our *auf wiedersehen* floating in the night air back to those wonderful girls who had brought some degree of comfort to a cold and hungry group of men. We gave them our blessings as the train gathered speed and disappeared into the darkness.

We were on the train for five days and six nights, passing through Innsbruck on the way. To the south of Berlin we were shunted into a siding while an air raid was in progress; we could hear heavy-calibre bombs searching for their targets.

We sped eastwards. The journey seemed endless, but finally we arrived at our destination not far from the Polish border.

3
Lamsdorf

The winds blow in from the East and West,
Bringing the smoke from a thousand guns.
It's just a prelude to man's final test,
With the passing away of a million sons.

What a motley, unwashed crew we were as we jumped down from our trucks and were marched away to a huge POW camp. We had no clue where we were, except that we had travelled the last two or three days in an easterly direction towards Poland.* The guards told us that we were at a place called Lamsdorf, near Breslau; the camp was Stalag 344.

Once through the gates, we were lined up and checked as to name, number and rank by a German NCO. Beside him stood an English sergeant major; off to one side was the camp Kommandant. When the check was finished, we were detailed off under our hut commanders (generally warrant officers or sergeants), then marched away to the huts and allocated our bunks. These bunks were of wooden construction, in pairs one above the other, with wooden slats and straw palliasses for us to sleep on.

After roll-call the following morning, Dave, Bill and I went for a stroll round the camp and were amazed at its size. We found out it held over 10 000 men — Canadians, Poles, Indians, French, British, Australians, New Zealanders and Americans who had come in from all the different battlefields of Europe and North Africa. Among them were a lot of Air Force personnel who had been shot down.

The discipline in this camp was fairly strict, as I suppose it had to be with such large numbers of men. The daily routine started with a morning parade and a roll-call in each hut, after which we had a snack, generally made from corn, and were issued with our lunch, a loaf of black bread for each two men and *Leberwurst* (liver sausage, which was mainly in

---

* Until the end of the Second World War, Germany's eastern boundary extended deep into territory that is now Polish — up to 200 km into the south-eastern corner of the country, where Chapters 3 and 4 are set.

the form of paste in a tube). Each day men from different huts were detailed for camp fatigues such as cleaning out the latrines and going into the pine forests nearby to collect wood for the kitchen stoves.

One morning, Bill, who had been outside walking round the camp, came in, sat down alongside Dave and me on the bottom bunk, and said quietly, 'I've got some latrine news for you two'.

'Well,' said Dave, 'don't keep us in suspense. Spill the beans'.

'I've just heard,' said Bill, 'that a tunnel is being dug under one of the huts. It's organised by the Air Force boys, but the exact hut is being kept a dead secret'.

There and then we three decided to try and get in on this escape project, but try as we may, we could not find out who the head blokes were. So as winter was fast approaching, we resigned ourselves to wait until the following spring and summer, for we knew that our chances of escape would be well nigh impossible in the ice and snow.

Early one morning, not long after this, I heard a lot of yelling and commotion, and into our hut raced a German NCO, saying in a loud voice to our hut commander, 'Aufstehen, aufstehen, sie müssen hinaus gehen.' Seems I'd heard that somewhere before.

'Everyone outside,' said our hut sergeant.

So we all trooped out to see the guards lined up, rifles at the ready, and the Kommandant shouting orders. Standing off to one side were two guards holding two big Alsatians. One of the boys who'd been in the camp for some time told us that this was the usual procedure for a camp search.

Into each hut stamped the Kommandant, accompanied by the two guards with the Alsatians. Suddenly there was a shout and a lot of activity around a hut further up the line, and shortly after, the Kommandant came hurrying out and spoke to the sergeant in charge of the hut, who was then marched down to the Kommandant's office.

Well, what a turn for the books, or should I say for the Germans. We heard later that the boys digging the tunnel were bloody unlucky. They had dug right out under the barbed wire perimeter, but a couple of guards patrolling round the outside of the barbed wire felt the ground give way under their feet, and bang went the escape effort. What rotten luck!

*   *   *

The winter came slowly at first, but by Xmas the snow was deep upon the ground, and we did our best to enjoy ourselves. We sang carols, thought of our folks back home, and enjoyed the Red Cross parcels, which had small Xmas cakes and plum puddings in them. God bless the Red Cross! Our families had also sent special gifts — lovely, warm, hand-knitted socks, scarves and balaclavas, all made from fair dinkum Aussie wool, and believe me, how we sent our prayers to our loved ones way down in that sunny southland.

Through January and February the blizzards came sweeping in from the east across the plains of Poland from the Russian steppes. The Aussies and (especially) the Indians, who were not used to European winters, felt the cold far more than the English and the Americans. We reckoned that the blizzards came from as far away as the frozen tundras of remote Siberia.

In one of the huts, some brains had made a wireless receiving set. Don't ask me where they got the parts; suffice it to say, however, that one of the boys in each hut would go out each evening and return with a fairly comprehensive account of the situation on the various battle fronts. Our news gatherer was a chap named Bob Della who kept us on tenterhooks while he slowly imparted the latest information to us. He would become exasperated when some of the boys asked him to repeat the news, but then good naturedly agreed to their requests.

We could see that the tide of war was turning in the Allies' favour, with the Russians coming in from the east and the large industrial cities of Germany being laid waste by the Allied Air Force. We knew that a second front, with a landing in Europe, could not be far away.

The cold grew very intense. It was a grim winter, and we heard that there were train-loads of frost-bitten German troops who had lost hands and feet coming in from the Russian front.

We heard a story about the Russian POW camp not far to the east of us. As the story goes, the Germans put Alsatian guard dogs in between the two outer rings of barbed wire around the perimeter of the camp. In the morning, the only pieces left of those dogs were their bones, the Russians having eaten the flesh and made moccasins out of the skins, such was their deplorable state of hunger. When it came to the Russians, the Germans did not recognise the International Red Cross.

Those of us lucky enough not to be registered for camp duties spent most of the day lying on our bunks fully clothed, with our socks on and covered by blankets, and even then it was freezing. Sometimes the blizzards blew continuously for days on end, and heavy snow covered the camp. Looking out from our hut windows through the barbed wire, when the fierce winds had eased, we could see the beautiful pines with their branches weighed down by the gently falling snow, and it reminded me of scenes in films I'd seen back home. Even from where I stood, I was impressed by the beauty of the scene.

*   *   *

What's in a name? Well, none of us are responsible for attaching a name tag to our bodies — it's our parents who do this for us — and I have often seen kids at school suffer for the names well-meaning parents give their children.

I took a fair bit of chiacking at school, but being young it rolled off my back like water from a duck's. In the army, some of the blokes called me Broody, à propos of chook, and since then I've had letters addressed to me as Mr. Brindle-Woods, à propos of cow, but what topped the lot was when I submitted a letter to an editor of a Sydney paper, and it was returned addressed to a Mr. Briedwell-Woods! Well, I ask you!

You might say, what has all this got to do with the state of affairs in a prison camp? Well, hang on, let me tell you. I happened to be one of those unlucky so and so's allotted to do camp duties, and we were lined up outside our huts. The German Feldwebel (sergeant), who spoke fairly good English, was detailing the various jobs when I heard him call: 'Brudenell, you will go out in the Woods with the working party'. Hell, I thought this beats the bloody band, but I didn't argue, and some of us were issued with small handsaws, and then we were marched out the front gate through the falling snow.

I thought of the Teddy Bears' Picnic, but we didn't go out in the Woods to play. We struggled through snow up to our knees, and when we got into the forest, we pulled dead branches out of the snow, sawed them into two-foot lengths, and tied them into bundles to carry back to camp.

*   *   *

I don't think I would be wrong were I to say that amongst the many thousands of POWs in the camps scattered around Europe, the great majority had their high days and their low days. When the low days took over, you would see men walking round the inside perimeter of the camp hour after hour. One did not have to ask them what was in their thoughts, you knew what the answer would be — home, family, and your pals fighting and dying so that one day you might walk out those front gates a free man. You became terribly introverted, a certain amount of frustration and self pity took over, and you tried to walk it all out of your system. I've seen some men go over the edge and end up in the camp hospital, but had we known what was happening in those shocking death camps almost alongside us, in the infamous Japanese POW camps, and along the horror stretch of the Burma railway, where I lost two of my best mates, we would have thought we were living in luxury. But everything is relevant, and it is of the moment that most people are concerned, especially when things are not going too well.

One day I was having one of those moments when my spirits were at a fairly low ebb. I was tramping through the snow round the perimeter of the camp, when something happened to me that I am sure must be experienced by most people at least once in their lives, just when it's needed.

A hand fell on my shoulder, and a voice tinged with a Scottish accent said, 'Hold on there Basil,' and on turning round, I saw this Scotsman from my hut, standing there with a grin on his face. He was one of those men who have an air of tranquillity, who never seem to be ruffled. He managed a tea plantation in Assam, India, and had the same calm philosophy as the people of that country.

He went on to say, 'I could see you were having one of those days, Basil, but just remember this: everything passes, and one day you will look back and think of this as just another episode in what I hope will be a long and happy life.'

'Thanks, Scotty,' I said, 'but come the summer, if I don't get out of this situation, it won't be for want of trying.'

His reply — 'I understand what you mean, and I wish you the best of luck, Basil, but take care' — was said with all sincerity. You know, it is that hand on the shoulder when one needs it, that means more than all the money in the world.

*   *   *

When spring comes, can summer be far behind? The snow and ice began to thaw, and quite a few of us volunteered for the various working parties around the country. Some of the jobs were on farms and others in small factories. One's chances of escape were far better on the outside of the main camp.

One day, not long after the snow and ice had melted, I was sloshing through the mud when I noticed a crowd round the big pool in the centre of the camp. The pool was there for the express purpose of dousing any fires that might start in our huts and was, I might add, just about frozen solid in winter.

Pushing through the mob, I looked into the pool, and to my surprise and astonishment saw a body with a rope round its neck. To the rope was attached a fairly big stone.

'Poor bugger, he must have committed suicide,' said a bloke near me.

'Why the hell wasn't he posted missing?' said another.

'Well, that's a good question, maybe they wanted to keep it quiet,' said the sergeant in charge of our hut.

Well, it was not long before the camp Kommandant and some guards arrived on the scene, and after a lot of shouting and commands, the body was taken away. We were all lined up outside our huts whilst the Feldwebel and hut commanders did a thorough check of our names and numbers. As it turned out, no one was missing from among the thousands of POWs in the camp.

Some time later, we heard through the underground, or what was known as the shit-house news, that the drowned person was a German spy who had been planted in the camp with the incoming prisoners. He spoke half a dozen languages, and as each batch of recently captured prisoners came in from the various battle fronts, he would mix in with them, trying to discover information of use to the Germans. I cannot vouch for the authenticity of this story, but if true, we must have had some tough men in the camp.

*   *   *

All through that winter, Dave, Bill and I held confabs about escaping and about which direction to take, Dave suggesting we make for Switzerland, whereas Bill and I voted for Yugoslavia and Tito's partisans, or our own forces in Italy. Finally Bill and I won out, and it was decided that if we heard of a factory or farm to the south looking for labour, we would volunteer.

I said to the boys one day, 'You know, if we could get to the Danube, we could steal a boat, row down through Hungary and Romania at night, cross the Black Sea to Turkey, and then cross Syria to our own forces in Palestine.'

There was dead silence, and then Bill said with an anxious tone in his voice, 'Basil, do you feel all right?'

At the same time, Dave had an incredulous look on his face. 'Basil,' he said, 'you must be off your cotton pickin' head. Do you realise how far that is?'

'No matter,' I said, 'it would save us a bloody lot of walking.'

'Got any more brilliant ideas?' said Bill, with what I thought was a slight touch of sarcasm in his voice.

Our spirits were buoyed up when we heard of a small factory somewhere to the south that wanted some POWs to work there, so we three put our names down on the list, and it wasn't long before we were told to be ready to move on the following day.

Much to our sorrow, Dave became very sick with a bad dose of flu and our hut commander scratched his name off the work detail, but not before Dave had volubly protested that he was fit and well. However, I think he realised that he was too weak to go, and although he was bitterly disappointed, he promised to try and join us later.

After our midday snack the following day, our hut sergeant told Bill, me and two other men to collect our belongings and fall in outside. We went to say goodbye to Dave, who was lying on his bunk looking pretty sick and miserable.

'Hard luck, Dave,' said Bill, as we shook hands. 'It's only a temporary parting, you old bugger.'

'See you soon, Dave, ol' pal,' I said with a grin, trying to cheer him up, but deep inside I felt the parting, as we had been mates for a long time. Bill and I turned at the door to wave goodbye, not knowing at the time that it would be well over a year before we would see Dave again, in Sydney.

At long last we were on our way, and I hoped we would travel a damn sight further than where we were being taken. We were marched through the camp and put in a big brick building near the front gate. Around the walls, and in rows down the middle of the room, were a large number of bunks, and selecting one each, we threw our belongings on the end and lay down, expecting to be called in the next hour or two. But we were not moved that day and spent the night in this barrack room, whiling away the time listening to the comments of our fellow travellers and wondering about our destination.

On the walls, those who had gone before and returned to this camp had scribbled dozens of messages and comments on conditions in the various work camps, such as 'Bloody good farm, plenty of eggs and poultry, farmer's daughter makes a good lay in the haystack!' or 'Camp Kommandant a real bastard,' and so on, and accompanying each message was the name of the work camp.

Early next morning we were roused from our bunks, given a meal, assembled outside in three ranks with guards on either side and to the rear, and marched out the front gate. After walking some distance to the railway siding, we were entrained in cattle trucks for another unknown destination.

4

Krnov

The moonlight shines on the factory site,
As four men stand by the hole in the wall.
Their one main thought a successful flight,
For this is their answer to freedom's call.

JUNE 1944. We rattled away down the line heading south. Inside the truck a dozen or more of us sat in the semi-darkness with our backs against the walls. Here I was on the move again, but I knew that I was not the only one in this predicament. At any one time during the war there must have been thousands of POWs and slave-labour men and women in similar circumstances, jammed into boxcars and cattle trucks trundling their way across Europe, carrying their human cargo to the many factories, farms and coal mines scattered throughout the continent.

Bill and I sat next to one another and we knew in our hearts that this was a do-or-die attempt to escape. Taking a look at my fellow travellers, and listening to their desultory conversation and quaint country accents, I guessed that most of them were English, except for one tall fellow who had a decidedly Scottish accent, and a shorter, tough-looking bloke whom Bill and I found out later to be a Kiwi. Little did we know then that these two men would play a vital role in our escape, and that one would have to go a long way to find two such tough and reliable men.

I was awakened from my reverie as the train jolted to a sudden stop. Looking out through the iron bars of the window, we could see a platform and what looked like a big waiting shed. There was the sound of bolts being drawn on the outside of the heavy wooden door of our truck, and next thing the door slid back and the guards were yelling, 'Aufstehen, aufstehen, schnell, schnell,' at the same time beckoning us outside and pointing to the large shed. So we filed out, trooped across to the shed, and going through the large opening, seated ourselves on the hard wooden benches round the walls.

'Hello, what have we here?' said the tough-looking Kiwi, who was sitting alongside Bill, in a very quiet voice. He took a quick look around to make sure the guards were outside, got up and walked over to one corner, where on the wall was tacked what looked like a very old map covered in dust. He quickly pulled it from the wall, folded it and shoved it in his pocket.

'You never know, it might come in handy,' he said.

Bill and I exchanged glances, and Bill whispered to me quietly, 'Looks as though he is one of our mob.'

The chap must have overheard Bill, for he introduced himself, saying simply, 'I'm Gordon,' and with a knowing grin added, 'If you blokes mean what I think you mean, you can count me in on any scheme you have in mind'.

'More about that later, Gordon, when we get settled in our new quarters,' I said quietly, and he gave an understanding nod, sat back in his seat, and remained quiet.

The guards told us the name of the railway junction was Neisse, and that we would have to wait for another train to take us south. 'The further the better,' said Bill in a subdued voice, but it was nearly two hours before a goods train pulled into the platform and we were herded into a boxcar attached to the rear of the train.

Towards late afternoon the train came to a stop at a small siding, and the all-too-familiar cry of 'Aufstehen, aufstehen, hinausgehen' rang out as the bolts to our door were drawn. Jumping down, we were formed into two ranks, and with guards keeping a watchful eye, we were marched towards a group of buildings about 200 yards away. Going in through two big wooden gates, we noticed on our left a one-storey building about 100 feet in length, consisting of several rooms with iron bars over the windows. Crowding the doorway of the first room, and peering through the windows, were a number of women; we found out later they were Ukrainian.

We were brought to a halt and told to turn right. Looking around, we found ourselves completely surrounded by a very large square. To the right and in front of us were what appeared to be cement-rendered brick buildings; to our left and behind us were two long one-storey buildings.

So this was the square from which we would have to escape! Bill and I took a good look round for future reference.

We became aware of the sound of voices and a lot of giggling above our heads, and looking up at the two-storey buildings on the right side of the square, we could see the heads and shoulders of a lot of women, who were gazing down on us from the windows above and waving. Of course the boys waved back and blew kisses to them, and some wag chimed in with 'Gord lumme chum, what 'ave we 'ere, beaut bits of fluff, ain't we 'alf gonna 'ave some fun?'

We were brought smartly to attention by our squad leader and addressed by a German in civilian clothes, obviously someone in authority.

'This is your work place,' he said in clipped tones. 'If you work well, you will be treated well. If not, you will be returned immediately to your main camp. That is all I have to say for the moment.' And with that he strode away to his quarters at the far end of the building containing the women, who were still looking down on us.

Our two new guards, Franz and August, took over. They were to be our regular night-shift guards and consequently would play an important part in our plans for escape. We were shown to our sleeping quarters, the third room in the long building on our left as we came through the gates of the factory. It was a room about 20 feet by 30, with iron bars on the windows and two-tiered bunks around the walls. In the centre of the room was a small table about six feet by three. Choosing our bunks, we dumped our gear and wandered out to make an inspection of our new surroundings.

Outside our room a passageway led from the front entrance to the back of the building. The rear door opened on to a barbed-wire enclosed area in which was situated an outside lavatory.

Across the passageway opposite our room a large solid door opened into our messroom, which held two large tables. There was a partition right along the far side of the messroom, stopping about three feet short of the ceiling; behind it were metal cupboards about six feet high, in which we stored our Red Cross parcels. The door to this area was locked every night, as was the door to our mess room. As we found out later, our boots were taken away from us every evening and placed in the mess room, and we were then locked in our sleeping quarters for the night.

That evening, before lights out, we sat around on our bunks; others played cards at the table in the centre of the room. We got to know one another a lot better on that first night. Our new friends included the two men who were to play an important part in our escape: the tall Scotsman, who said, 'Och mon, just call me Scotty,' and the tough-looking Kiwi named Gordon Fallis, whom we had met in the waiting shed.

What a great bunch of blokes they were. Some had been POWs since Dunkirk, and were still able to crack jokes and laugh heartily despite their long incarceration. Bill and I had decided not to broach our intention to escape until we got to know our workmates better, but we need not have worried, as we were quite impressed by the soldier companions who were to be our partners in crime.

Early next morning we were awakened as our door opened and August, the new guard, shouted, 'Aufstehen, aufstehen.' Our squad leader told us to get up and stand by our bunks, while the man who had addressed us on our arrival the day before took a count and had a good look at the bars on our windows.

Once our bunks were tidy, two men were detailed to go to the kitchen to draw our rations and bring them back to the mess room. One of the men dished into our dixies a thick gruel that seemed to consist of ground-up corn with lentils and vegetables in it. The other man poured from a big urn into our mugs the blackest of black coffee, made, so we heard, from burnt wheat; he also handed out our midday meal, consisting of one small loaf of black bread (rumour had it that a percentage was sawdust — we reckoned 75%), a tube of ersatz butter (supposedly made from coal), some *Leberwurst* (liver sausage) and a small square of cheese.

Seeing that our boots had been put in the mess room the night before, Bill and I made a detailed study of the room and particularly of the area behind the partition, where the iron cupboards holding our Red Cross parcels were pushed against the wall.

After washing our dixies and mugs at a tap out the back, we assembled in the big square in front of our barracks and were detailed to various jobs in and around the factory, our squad leader taking his orders from the same man who had checked our numbers in our sleeping quarters that morning.

Bill, Scotty and I were assigned to help a beautiful Russian girl who drove a table-top wagon pulled by two oxen. We proceeded out through the two big wooden factory gates, which were thrown open by one of the guards on the day shift. He did not come with us, but stood at the gate watching as we moved slowly towards the railway siding where we had arrived the day before.

The three of us sat dangling our legs over the end of the wagon as we approached the railway trucks, which were standing there waiting for us to unload the hundreds of bales of flax that arrived every week from other parts of Czechoslovakia and even, we were told, from as far away as Hungary.

When we reached the trucks, Natasha (as she indicated was her name) jumped up to give us a hand with the unloading, and disappearing inside, she started heaving the bales out of the truck. Bill and I never a chance to help her, for big Scotty leapt into the truck ahead of us, telling us he would help Natasha, and that we two could stay on the wagon to stack the bales. From the moment we got on the wagon, Bill and I could tell from Scotty's remarks that he had a decided admiration and a barely hidden desire for Natasha.

'This looks interesting,' said Bill. 'I wonder how long it will be before he tries to get her pants down?'

In the truck, meanwhile, Scotty, although working hard at rolling the bales out to Bill and me, was at the same time busy making passes at Natasha by giving her pats on the bottom, then putting both arms round the girl and trying to give her a kiss.

'Aha!' said Bill. 'What did I tell you?'

Natasha struggled furiously and fetched Scotty a big wallop on the side of the jaw. We could hear his 'ouch' from the wagon, so we guessed it must have hurt.

In the meantime, Bill and I were keeping a wary eye on the guard who, seeing that the bales weren't being unloaded, probably had an inkling of what was going on in the truck and started to move across towards us.

'Look out Scotty,' we cried, and the struggling ceased and the bales of flax came rolling out on to the table-top.

'I don't know whether you were just trying to kiss her or sow your wild oats, you old bugger,' said Bill with a grin, 'but you know the penalty for putting any woman in the family way and hindering Hitler's war effort.'

Scotty muttered something about not giving a bloody damn about the war effort, and he was only just having a bit of fun. We finished loading the wagon, and climbing on top, sat down on the bales, Scotty of course quite close to Natasha, who completely ignored him as she plied her whip over the backs of the oxen. In this way we slowly returned to Arbeits kommando 768, a small rope and paper factory near the town of Krnov* on the Czech-German border.

About three nights later, as Bill and I were sitting on our bunks, we were approached by the squad leader in charge of our working party.

'Well, you blokes,' he said, 'what have you got up your sleeves? The other day, when we first arrived, I noticed what a great interest you two were taking in the layout of the mess room and surrounds.'

There was dead silence. All talking ceased and heads turned in our direction. 'Now don't be worried,' he said. 'If you intend trying to escape,

* In my diary it is spelt Kunau, as pronounced in our working party.

47

I for one will give you every possible assistance, and I'm sure I speak for all the others.'

By this time most of the men in the room had crowded round our bunk. Bill and I looked at one another, then Bill nodded his head at me. 'That was our express purpose for coming to this working party,' I said, 'and if any of you would care to join us, you are quite welcome.'

There was a buzz of excitement and our squad leader held up his hand for silence. 'Make it quiet you blokes, or we will have the guards getting suspicious,' he said. Without exception, all of them promised to aid us in our plans for escape. Quite a few wanted to join in our scheme, amongst them the tall Scotsman and the tough-looking Kiwi.

*   *   *

When we had settled into the routine of the place and moved around in the various jobs, we soon got to know most of the Germans with whom we would be working, and believe me there were some queer characters amongst them. In charge of the whole show was the Direktor, a very remote figure who hardly spoke to anyone, but who ran the place with an iron hand. On the factory floor was this big buxom blonde, Frau Bischer, who appeared to be in charge of checking the rolls of paper and coils of rope as they came off the machines. With the aid of Atlas, an immensely strong young man, some of the boys would then wheel the paper and rope away on trolleys to the *Packerei* (packing department), where the Polish and Ukrainian girls worked. In charge of this big storage room were two German women, Freda and Emma.

Needless to say, some of the boys got a bit fresh with the women workers, and on passing them would give them friendly slaps on the bottom and feeling caresses, which were not altogether rebuffed. It was quite amusing to see how annoyed and angry Freda and Emma became if they saw this kind of nonsense going on, but perhaps they were a little envious.

As the bales of flax and bundles of cardboard and old paper came in, they were loaded into a lift and taken up to the storage floor, which was run by a bloke whom we nicknamed 'Sauerkraut'; with him was his offsider, whom we called 'Grim Jim'. These were two of the most uncommunicative specimens you could meet, and their only reply to our questions was a deep grunt.

Wherever we worked in the factory, we were continually watched by a character we called 'the Shadow,' who seemed to have no job in particular. The boys soon had his measure and we plied him with questions in our bastard German, which he greeted with a scowl, seeming to be quite annoyed.

Then there were two trash collectors whom we named 'Donner' and 'Blitzer'. They came in every day driving an old horse and cart, and their movements were so slow that every time they stopped, we expected horse, cart and drivers to collapse in one big heap. And of course we had an Adolphe, whose imitation of his leader — moustache and all — was a pretty good likeness. He never stopped praising Hitler whenever he had a chance to corner one of us POWs.

Another character was a wizened-up little bloke we named 'Red Eyes,' who seemed to be in charge of the machinery. He appeared to have a perpetual hangover, for whenever he came near, or spoke to us, he smelled to high heaven of stale beer. His offsider was a kindly old chap called Pop Schank, who spoke fairly good English; he told us it was a very sad day when Germany and Britain went to war against each other, and that our real enemy was Russia, who would one day try to rule the world with its communist doctrines.

On the other hand, we had a dyed-in-the-wool pro-Russian, communist to the core, who when he mentioned Hitler, would scowl, spit on the floor, angrily draw his finger across his throat, and point to the ground. After this he would look around furtively, to make sure he was not being watched, then put his fingers to his lips to ensure silence. We knew quite well that if he was heard, he would end up with lead poisoning. By way of passing, I must mention that he worked in the large machine shop, a place that had an important bearing in our plans for the eventual breakout.

That first week in our new quarters reminded me very much of the old army barracks back at Ingleburn, near Sydney, as it was a settling-in period, a time of getting to know your fellow men. When the key to our door was finally turned each night, we were locked up not only in the physical sense, but also with our thoughts, and it was as though the four walls of our room had been put there to contain and listen to all our varied stories and tales of home, our wishes, hopes and desires.

We came to know a lot about each other, and lying on our bunks in the darkness after lights out, we would discuss many topics. Most of us would reminisce, telling the rest of the boys about our homes, our families, our work back in our own countries, and then some wag would chime in with the old army joke that when he got home to his wife or girlfriend, the second thing he would do would be to take off his pack! And of course we had the usual bragging Don Juan, who would regale us with his many escapades — the way he dived out windows, clutching his pants in one hand and his shoes in the other, just avoiding the untimely arrival of some unsuspecting husband.

How I used to enjoy listening to the tales of those English blokes, with their fascinating county accents and their descriptions of quaint English villages, customs going back hundreds of years, and the wonderful antiquities of that grand old city, London.

We certainly missed those clandestine bulletins from the hidden radio back at the main camp at Lamsdorf, which gave us news of the fighting on the various battle fronts. It had been a great boost to our morale to hear that the tide of war was at last turning in the Allies' favour and that the enemy was gradually being pushed back on all fronts.

*   *   *

The tension in our barracks was building up. Each night we held long discussions about our escape plans, but when Bill and I told the boys that we intended making for Italy or Yugoslavia to join up with our own forces or Tito's partisans, their early enthusiasm waned somewhat. They thought it was a madcap scheme and too bloody far. As for crossing Hungary, our chances were mighty slim.

Finally our numbers dwindled to four. The tough-looking Kiwi said, 'I'm in on this. You blokes can include me in this stunt. It's why I came to work at this factory,' and Scotty spoke up too: 'Aye mon, ye maun count me in, ye canna gang awa' wi'out me'.

The leader of our working party spoke up. 'You have my word that I will give you every assistance, and I know I speak for the rest of these men.'

There was a general chorus of assent as the boys gathered round the four of us and either shook our hands or slapped us on the back. I guess I had a lump in my throat as I thought what a great lot of blokes these men were, when every single one of them, without exception, gave us his word to help us in our escape. I could tell by the look on their faces and the sincerity with which they spoke, that we had a good team.

At first we had no set plan of escape, so as we moved around the various jobs, we familiarised ourselves with our surroundings and all the likely avenues of escape. We studied the layout of the buildings, the gates, and most importantly, the guards, whose hours of duty were very long. When we first arrived, there appeared to be only two guards on day duty and two for the night watch. It was the latter who interested us most, so we did our best to be on good terms with August and Franz, the guards on duty at night.

After discussing a number of options, we came to the conclusion that the obvious place to make a break-out was the mess room, especially as our boots were taken away from us each night and placed in that room till parade next morning. We finally came up with the idea of making a hole in the wall behind the iron cupboards, working on it during our free time before being locked up for the night, when we had access to the area.

Every afternoon, when our work was finished, we were allowed to stroll for an hour or two in the big open area enclosed by the surrounding buildings, and also to go to the latrine out the back. Franz and August would unlock the door to our mess room and the door in the partition, to allow us to get a snack from our Red Cross parcels in the big iron cupboards. Later, two of our men would take two large iron saucepans to collect the evening meal, which was almost a replica of breakfast.

But what to do with the bricks and mortar from the hole?

Fortunately, the latrine out the back was very similar to the old country dunnies back in Australia; it consisted of a hole in the ground with a seat and a shelter on top. What more convenient place could we have to dump our ill-gotten gains?

After lights-out each night we kept a constant watch on the guards through the iron bars of our window, taking particular notice of their patrols round our sleeping quarters and especially the change of shifts. One night, I was keeping watch, when much to my surprise, round about ten or half past, the guard on the first shift stopped outside their sleeping quarters, which were next to ours, and taking a good look around, reached in through the outside door, lifted a chair from inside and bringing it out, placed it against the wall between our window and the guard room door. Then seating himself, he pulled out his pipe and tobacco and proceeded to puff away to his heart's content.

I couldn't believe my eyes. What a God-sent opportunity. I quickly alerted the other three, who, taking turns, sneaked quietly over to the window to have a look. It was just on an hour before the guard got up and went in to wake his relief. Our joy knew no bounds. Excitement was running high as we waited to see if the ritual would be repeated the following night. Sure enough, he carried out the same procedure and took about as long over his smoko.

Before we could get through that hole in the wall, however, we had to overcome two obstacles, namely the wood-panelled door to our sleeping quarters and the solid wooden door to our mess room. For the next two weeks it was to be day and night work if we were to break through to the outside world, but we were committed and our determination did not waver as we set about solving the problems that lay ahead.

Sunday was our rest day, or *freier Sonntag*, as the Germans called it. We were expected to clean our sleeping quarters and mess room, and just before the midday meal we were treated to a large mug of Lowenbrau beer, which we had to drink at the back of our quarters, inside the wire enclosure. This barbed-wire and mesh fence ran the whole length of our barracks and enclosed the exercise yard behind the Ukrainian women's sleeping quarters. We were, of course, kept at bay by a stoutly constructed fence of the same type that ran along the back between us and the women, who, I might mention, also received a beer ration.

On the Sunday following the little fracas between Natasha and Scotty, we were walking up and down drinking our beer, while some of the boys ogled the girls, blew kisses, and made such remarks as, 'Boy, if I could get her into bed for the night, I'd give her something to remember me by'.

Scotty's attention was focused mainly on Natasha. Calling her by name, he raised his mug and drank her health, and to our amazement, Natasha walked over to the fence and standing on tiptoe, she handed her beer to Scotty through the barbed wire at the top of the fence. There was a roar from the boys, and did they give Scotty one hell of a ribbing, but the look of surprise and pleasure on his face was a picture to behold.

That very afternoon, an incident occurred that may well have cost Scotty his life. Every Sunday afternoon, three or four of Hitler's brownshirt soldiers used to cycle down from an army barracks a few miles away, and riding into the square, would prop their bikes against the Polish women's quarters, which they entered with quite a swagger, and proceed to satisfy their sexual desires with the poor women, who had to submit to their will.

Well this day, a German NCO happened to notice Natasha, who was standing at the door of the Ukrainian women's quarters, and he beckoned her over, at the same time pointing to the Polish women's barracks. Seeing this, Scotty raced over with his fists closed, but quick as a flash the NCO went for the big Luger pistol in the holster strapped on the belt round his waist. Bill and I, seeing the danger Scotty was in, raced over and grabbed an arm each and between us managed to drag him away, persuading him how foolish it was. Believe me, it was no easy task to hold back a wild and furious Scotsman.

By this time the German had yanked the pistol from its holster, and shouting angrily, was pointing it menacingly at the boys, and in particular at Scotty. With his other arm, he pointed in the direction of our quarters, and we could see that if we did not obey his orders, he would start using the Luger, so we quietly and quickly retreated to our barracks, and while some of us watched the German through the window, the rest of us made Scotty realise how foolish was his rash action, for we knew that the German NCO would not have hesitated to use the pistol, had Scotty got close enough to strike him. After a short time, however, the German cooled down, re-holstered his pistol, and strode into the Polish women's barrack, shrugging his shoulders as if dismissing the whole affair.

That night in our sleeping quarters, we four, plus the leader of our working party and a few others, held a round-table conference as to when we should make a start on our plan of escape. We decided to begin work on the hole in the wall the following afternoon, when we had knocked off work. There was an air of excitement and expectation amongst the boys in the room, and they promised their whole-hearted cooperation, thinking of ways and means of assisting us in our efforts.

The following day, Monday, was one of the worst I experienced in the whole time I was working in the factory. We were detailed to clean rust from the inside of some old boilers about ten feet long by four to five feet in diameter. Four of us were selected to do the job, which entailed climbing down through a hole in the top of the boiler just big enough for a person to squeeze through.

Only two people at a time could work in this confined space, and it was impossible to stand upright when we were using hammers to belt the rust from the inside surface. We were each issued with a small mask, but they were perfectly useless, for they only just covered the mouth and nose, and continually slipped from our faces during the work. An electric light globe was suspended on a lead through the opening at the top. You can well imagine the deafening noise inside that hollow tube; when combined with the dust, it put a limit on the time we could work in the chamber. After half an hour we had had enough, and changed places with those waiting outside.

That afternoon, when we had knocked off work, the boys let the four conspirators have our showers first, in the small washroom off the passageway leading to the back of the building. The room had a concrete floor, a shower in one corner, and a concrete tub in the other for washing our clothes. Our ablutions finished, we strolled casually into the mess room and through the partition door, which we hurriedly closed behind us.

Outside the boys were playing their part. Some were in our immediate vicinity in the mess room, over by the windows, keeping watch on the rest of the boys, who in turn were keeping a wary eye on the guards, who seldom came into the barracks, though occasionally one or other of them would stroll through the passageway and out to the back. The boys outside were strolling up and down near the windows to the mess room, and as they went past we could hear them singing old nostalgic war songs such as 'Roll out the Barrel,' 'White Cliffs of Dover,' and 'There'll always be an England'. To these tunes they added a little ditty that some wag had thought up on the spur of the moment. It was quite suited to the time and place and went like this:

> Oh it's only a hole in the wall,
> But there's plenty of room for us all.
> When you're away and roaming free,
> That's where we all will long to be.

Of course whenever the guards were near, this little song faded away to a low murmur, and a switch to another song took place right smartly, with a warning whistle of approaching danger.

We had pulled the iron cupboard away from the wall and were waiting for the all-clear signal from the boys in the mess room. The atmosphere was tense. Standing there looking at the other three, I wondered if they felt the same surge of excitement and expectancy as I did.

'OK boys, all clear,' came a voice from the mess room.

'Let's get stuck into this bloody hole,' said Gordon quietly. To our surprise, Bill casually took a piece of chalk from his pocket and drew a large circle on the wall about chest-high, big enough to allow our shoulders to pass through.

'Good thinking, Bill,' I said. 'The old grey matter is working.' Bill's only reply was a non-committal grunt, but he was one of those chaps whose actions spoke louder than words.

And so a beginning was made on what we hoped would lead to our eventual path to freedom.

Having 'borrowed' a large sack and a sharp, pointed pick from the storeroom, we decided that Gordon and Scotty would start the hole, while Bill and I would hold a sack underneath, against the wall, to catch the rubble and prevent it making a noise falling to the floor.

The wall was nearly 18 inches thick and consisted of a layer of cement about two inches thick on both the outside and inside, enclosing the main body of the wall, which contained a conglomerate of sand, gravel and large round river stones, held together by a mixture of clay and mortar.

As Gordon set to with a will, followed in turn by the powerful Scotty, the only sound to be heard in that confined space was the noise of the pick. It was tough going through the outer layer of cement and it took two afternoons of solid hard work to make a hole in it big enough for our bodies.

That dunny out the back was really coming in handy now as Bill and I carried out our loads of rubble and tipped them down through the hole. One afternoon, when we were going out the back door carrying our load, the guard on patrol came round the outside of the barbed wire at the back. We held our breath, and Bill said in a low voice, 'Keep walking,' so we nonchalantly carried our load round to the dunny, went inside and emptied it down the hole, and marched straight back into the building. That guard must have thought we were having a clean-up inside our quarters, and how right he was.

Having picked through the cement, we were faced with this fairly solid conglomerate. Our biggest worry was the size of the large round stones, some as big as footballs, so you can well imagine how careful we had to be the further we penetrated.

There was a terrific undercurrent of excitement when we were locked in our quarters that first night. All the boys were discussing our progress on the hole. Their enthusiasm to help us in any way they could made us feel on top of the world and ever so grateful for their spontaneous offers of help, so there and then we decided to make a start on the first of the other two obstacles barring our way, namely the panels in the wooden door to our sleeping quarters.

About an hour before lights-out, we organised a singsong to cover up any noise we might make whilst working on the door. We had purloined a very sharp knife with a thick blade from the workshop, and with this we silently proceeded to ease off the long narrow wooden strips that ran down the sides and along the bottom of the panel, holding it in place. Once the strips were off, we put them back in place with thin tacks, covering any marks left showing with a stain the same colour as the wood (another prize from that very useful workshop).

While some of the boys were working on the panel, the four of us were busy plying needle and twine, making packs from old trousers, which we split down the seams, cut to shape, and sewed into four quite large packs so each of us could carry food, clothing, and a 'borrowed' German blanket.

What a great bunch of blokes those men were. Without their help, our escape may not have been possible; they pitched in 100 per cent, even though in their hearts they most likely envied us and our madcap plans.

They also gave us food from their Red Cross parcels, which contained such a wonderful variety of sustenance, and without which I feel sure many thousands of POWs would have died.

The other obstacle was the solid wooden door on the other side of the passage that separated our sleeping quarters from the mess room. We just had to have a key, but how to obtain it was another question. Miracles of miracles, however — you wouldn't believe it — one of the guards on the day shift, feeling the heat, used to take his jacket off and hang it on a nail outside the factory door before going on his rounds inside. Well it was only a matter of moments for one of us to get an imprint of the key in a soft cake of soap, and we soon had a perfect duplicate made out of old iron in that ever-handy and very convenient workshop.

About a week before our proposed breakout, we had a kind of farewell party, and what a shindig! The guards had let us keep a four-gallon drum in our sleeping quarters for they thought it a great joke when they heard for what purpose it was intended.

We were making home brew!

We three parts filled the drum with water, and for weeks had been adding prunes and raisins from our parcels. To some this might seem like a waste of good food, but we did it mainly to relieve the monotony, boredom and anxiety of our everyday work. When we thought the fermenting process had finished, we decided to give it a try, and the results were pretty devastating. What started out to be a quiet drinking party in our sleeping quarters, just before lights-out, turned into a wild, chaotic bedlam. We were like howling dervishes, and the more we drank, the wilder we became; I'll guarantee that bawdy army songs were never sung with such abandon.

Meanwhile the guards became very alarmed and began shouting at us and banging on our door with the butts of their rifles. There would be silence for a while, then some of us, in our maudlin state, would start to giggle, and that would be the signal for a fresh outburst of wild singing and shouting, followed by more crashing of rifle butts on our door. Finally that powerful brew got the better of us. More than half the boys were sick and the rest clung to the iron bars at the windows, taking in big gulps of fresh air.

What a sorry sight we were when we reported for work the next morning, bleary-eyed, some of the boys groaning and holding their heads, while the guards had big grins on their faces.

At last the final week arrived. Everything was in readiness and an undercurrent of excitement ran through us all as the packs were finished.

We had just about come to the cement on the outside of the hole in the wall when we came across a very large stone, the largest we had come across so far. We decided to leave it just in case.

On returning to our barracks after work one afternoon, only a few days before our attempt, we found a notice pinned to our door informing us that any prisoner caught trying to escape would be shot. Now this was a little worrying, to say the least, as we thought the guards might have got wind of something going on, but we came to the conclusion it was the invasion of France, which had just taken place, that was making the Germans jittery.

The good Lord must have been smiling down on me, as wonder of wonders, two days before our attempt, I received a parcel from my mother which contained a pound of block chocolate, wrapped in waterproof paper and sealed with tinfoil. Amazingly, the Germans had not opened the parcel, as they generally did. (Though to be fair, I don't think the chocolate would have been confiscated.) That must have cost the family quite a bit of scrounging and saving. God bless them.

We melted the chocolate and into it stirred the contents of four small tins of rolled oats from our Red Cross parcels. When the mixture had cooled down into a solid block, we cut it into four equal parts to add to the rest of the food in our packs.

*   *   *

WEDNESDAY, 28 JUNE 1944, the fateful day for our escape attempt, everything and everyone was ready for the hour of departure. After we had knocked off work that afternoon, we tried our duplicate key. To our dismay, nothing happened on our first attempt. Then one of the English chaps, who had some experience back home with a locksmith, suggested we try turning the key a second time, and to our relief the latch worked. Three cheers for a little knowledge at the right time and place.

The atmosphere was tense in the locker room. While some of the boys kept watch through the mess room windows for any signals from the rest of the boys outside (who themselves were strolling up and down keeping an eye on the guards and doing their stint of singing), we four were behind the partition. Having retrieved our packs from behind the iron cupboards, we proceeded to fill each of them with exactly the same quantity of food.

Into the packs also went underclothes, shirts, socks, jumpers and other odds and ends such as soap and toothbrushes, most of which had been sent from our folks back home, and of course last but not least the borrowed German blankets. When the packs were full, they must have weighed 40 pounds or more. Having finished the task, we shoved the packs away in the iron cupboards, hoping like hell the guards would not make a late inspection, which was sometimes the case.

*   *   *

At long last the moment had arrived. This was it, the hour we had worked towards with so much faith and hope in our hearts. There was a certain amount of tremor in the boys' voices as they sang farewell that night. We shook hands with all the boys, not without a feeling of sadness, for we had become firm friends over the past few weeks and knew that if we were successful in our bid for freedom, we would in all probability never see them again.

We could hear the heavy tramp of the guard's boots as he patrolled round our barracks, his every movement watched by a couple of the boys posted at the window next to the guards' sleeping quarters. We went over our final arrangements with the boys who were staying behind. We had worked out a plan whereby a long rope ran from the window next to the guards' sleeping quarters, out through the hole in our barrack room door, across the passage and through the open door of our mess room to the hole in the wall. One pull of the rope, and the guard had taken a chair from his quarters and sat down; two pulls, and he was lighting his pipe and settling in for his nightly rest; three pulls meant danger, don't go, return.

It was decided that since I was the smallest, I would go through the hole first, take the packs as they were handed to me by the others, place them against the wall, then go to the corner of the building nearest the guards. Bill, the next one through the hole, would go to the other corner, and we would both keep watch while the remaining two made their exit, grabbed their packs and bolted for the nearby stream, followed swiftly by Bill and me.

We had arranged with the leader of the working party to tell the Germans, when they discovered our absence, that we had gone to join our forces, who had just landed in France. When he asked us where we were really going, I jokingly replied, 'We are going home for Xmas'.

'No kidding Basil,' he said. 'Christ, you're a bloody optimist, but the best of British luck to you all,' at the same time giving each of us an encouraging slap on the back. (We were actually headed for Yugoslavia or Italy, but were more inclined towards the former, as it was by far the shorter route and only entailed crossing Hungary, after which we would try to link up with Tito's partisans.)

It was nearly 11 p.m. when we slipped through the hole in the door to our sleeping quarters, with the men's whispered good-byes and good lucks ringing in our ears.

*   *   *

We stood in the darkness, tense and alert, having hurriedly put on our boots and pulled the iron cupboard away from the wall to reveal that dark hole, the result of so much hard work, and through which lay all our hopes and desires and who knows what on the other side. To this day I can still see us poised in the darkness, our packs at our feet, Gordon with his hand holding the cord line, big Scotty standing by the hole waiting to move the last big stone, and Bill and I ready for instant action.

'One,' whispered Gordon, touching Scotty on the shoulder; 'two,' giving him another tap. We all waited tensely for that third tug on the line, and after a moment, when it did not arrive, Gordon pointed at the hole and whispered the fateful word: 'Go'.

Scotty reached in and put his hands on the stone, and no sooner did he try to pull it away than it slipped through his fingers and fell to the ground outside, along with all the cement covering the outside of the hole. Well, the noise the stone and cement made, we thought would alert not only the guard sitting on the chair, but also his sleeping partner.

Again we tensed ourselves, waiting for that third tug, and when it did not arrive, Scotty and Bill lifted me up and shoved me feet first through the hole. Landing on the pile of rubble, I quickly took the packs as they were handed to me, laid them against the wall, then raced to one corner to keep watch. Bill followed in the twinkling of an eye and ran to the other corner, whilst the other two, having scrambled through the hole, picked up their packs and made a dash for the nearby stream, closely followed by Bill and myself.

Just imagine what would have happened if we had moved that stone in the afternoon. All our plans would have been dashed to the ground.

5
Pines

Through the tall, dense forests we make our way,
Not a sound from our boots on the pinewoods floor.
For this is no time to linger and stay,
And our cherished hope to return here no more.

At the rendezvous by the creek, we adjusted our packs, and I turned to take a brief look at the dark cluster of buildings and that black hole in the wall, showing up in the moonlight. I could just imagine the scene back at the barracks, with the boys whispering to one another about our flight, wondering, not without qualms, what would happen to them once the hole was discovered. I sincerely hoped their treatment would not be too rough.

I was awakened from my reverie by the urgency in Bill's voice. 'Bloody hell, Basil, what the blazes do you think you're doing? Let's get out of here.'

'I'm with you Bill,' I said, 'but I was just thinking of our mates back there'.

'Don't worry about them,' said Bill, with sympathy in his voice. 'They'll be all right, let's look after ourselves.'

We got down in earnest to the business of putting as many miles as possible between ourselves and our pursuers. All that could be heard in the silence of the night was the splash of our boots as we waded up a shallow stream. By walking in the water we would, of course, throw off any tracker dogs that the Germans might put on our trail, sometimes the case for escaping prisoners.

We had timed the break-out to coincide with the half moon, for with the moon coming up to the full, we would have better walking conditions. We had decided to walk all night for the first two weeks and hide during the day until we were well clear of the search area and our pursuers.

After wading in the stream for what we judged to be about two miles, we swung to the south, guided by a very small compass that one of our Air Force friends had given us to help us on our way. We also used the

Pole or North Star to confirm the general direction in which we were headed.

We formed single file and almost immediately began climbing stiff, hilly country, which slowed our progress somewhat, especially with those hefty packs on our backs. We walked almost in silence on the dead pine needles, with moonlight filtering through the top branches of this beautiful forest and the fragrant scent of pines filling the air.

This was our first night of freedom in a long, long time, but we were a vast distance from our homeland, and I think that first night's march was the toughest of the whole trip; we never spared ourselves, slogging on mile after mile. On top of this we were all tensed up, and that, coupled with anxiety, added to the strain of the journey.

Eventually, after nearly five hours of hard going, and nearly dead-beat with exhaustion, we decided to camp for the night, so selecting a small grove of pines, we crawled into the middle of them and immediately fell sound asleep.

It was getting on towards midday when the sun's rays, streaming through the branches overhead, must have woken us up, but the sound of Scotty's voice whispering to us in a subdued warning tone to 'keep still' made us remain perfectly motionless, and we became aware of the whirring sound of a light aircraft circling overhead. We guessed that whoever was up there must be looking for us, as the plane kept searching for nearly an hour, backwards and forwards, working to a very thorough pattern, before disappearing into the distance. How we blessed those pines and their sheltering canopy.

I'll never forget that first morning of waking up and realising I was a free man. Instead of looking out through the iron bars of our sleeping quarters, here we were in the centre of this lovely forest, with the strong scent of pines in the morning air and the birds chirping away in joyous melody, and I said to myself, 'Sing on you little beauties,' as I thought of the old saying, 'as free as the birds'. Maybe we were now one of them.

Not far away we heard the sound of a stream running down the steep hillside, and crawling out from our cover, we walked over to find beautiful, clear water. Sloshing it over our faces and hands, we drank our fill, then replenished our water bottles and walked back to the packs.

We were mighty hungry, so you can imagine how we made short work of that part of our rations. (We had portioned our food to last at least two weeks.) Our meal consisted of a piece of the oatmeal block, followed by a large round Canadian biscuit somewhat like an Arnott's Sao back home, but twice as thick and about four inches in diameter; on these we put either a sprinkling of sultanas or a thin slice of bully beef. (All of this came from our Red Cross parcels.) We usually finished our meal with a drink of Canadian powdered milk mixed with the pure, clear water of these hillside streams, which seemed to be everywhere.

For the remainder of that first day, we just lazed about or sat and talked of the excitement of the last twelve hours. I know all of us were terribly tense and somewhat dazed to find ourselves wandering at large in a strange country, not knowing with any certainty what lay ahead.

'Can you picture the look on the guard's face when he saw that hole in the wall?' asked Gordon.

'Aye mon, that I can,' said Scotty.

'I don't know who'd get the bigger shock,' said Bill, 'him or his mate. Fancy being woken up to be told that kind of bloody news.'

'Well,' I said, 'I wouldn't be in their shoes for all the tea in China. Can you imagine the Kommandant when they went to report the escape? Can't you just see him ranting and raving at those two guards and swearing like a trooper?'

The Kommandant would probably be transferred immediately to the Russian front, as was often the case. What would happen to the two guards was anybody's guess, and as for our boys, it was the general rule that they would be returned to the main camp that same day. To this day, I have never heard what actually happened in that remote place so long ago. I often think of Scotty and Natasha and wonder what happened to her, and whether she missed him after our escape.

That first afternoon, Gordon produced the map he'd pulled from the wall of the railway shed at the siding at Neisse, and laid it on the ground. We all gathered round it in a circle and tried to work out our exact position in relation to the map. We estimated that we must be somewhere near the watershed of the Olomouc Valley, as the streams in our vicinity seemed to be running south.

Now this map was a great help, as on it was the railway system of Silesia, showing the lines going right down into Czechoslovakia. It also pinpointed the major towns, allowing us to detour round them and avoid being captured by the Gestapo.

Thursday night and early Friday morning, the 29th and 30th of June 1944, found us on the second stage of our march after leaving our temporary place of abode, Arbeits kommando 768, near the border of Sudetenland, on the night of Wednesday the 28th of June. On this second night, we were leaning against a haystack, having a rest, when suddenly a man appeared in front of us. To our relief, he spoke in broken English, and it turned out that he was a Magyar who had come from Hungary some years ago, and that this was his farm. We told him, also in broken English, that we were French, and heading east past Jägerndorf (Krnov), whereupon he pointed out the different points of the compass and the direction of nearby towns and railways.

He seemed friendly enough, but in our position we could not trust anyone. All strangers were suspect. We thanked him, and after saying goodbye, we strode away in the moonlight in an easterly direction. Looking back, I could still see him standing there, gazing in our direction, so once out of sight, we swung round to the south and kept going hard for about three hours over beautiful undulating clover and wheat country, and crossed the railway line near what we thought was the town of Freudenthal. We finally dropped down exhausted in another grove of those wonderful protecting pines at about 2.30 a.m.

The third night of our march we travelled through steady, soaking rain. The gear in our packs became sopping wet and consequently very heavy, but the beautiful country through which we were walking helped to take our minds off the unpleasant weather. We were also keyed up to the nth degree, and each of us had a determination to achieve the goal we had set ourselves, come what may.

We must have travelled about fifteen miles that night. Finally, dead beat and soaking wet, we crawled into a good cover of pines and fell into an exhausted sleep.

The next day we woke about nine o'clock to bright sunshine, with the sparkle of raindrops clinging to the pine needles, and birds whistling in the forest. We were hanging our clothes out to dry under the cover of the overhanging branches, chatting quietly to one another, when suddenly we froze into silence, alarmed by the frequent sounds of low barking in the forest around us. Keeping quite still, we soon found out that the barks came not from dogs, but from the many deer we could see wandering through the forest nearby.

Going by compass, map, and the North Star, we worked out our position to be somewhere near Kriegsdorf. The going was fairly tough on the fourth night of our march, in more ways than one, as firstly we came across a large viaduct spanning a wide gorge, across which ran a railway line.

What followed was one of those close encounters, or as one might say, narrow shaves, and it happened in the twinkling of an eye. In our hurried march we almost walked into a German patrol of about half a dozen men. Going to ground very smartly behind some low bushes, we took stock of our situation. In the bright moonlight, we could see soldiers patrolling the railway line on both sides of the viaduct and for some distance on either side of the gorge.

'Bloody hell, that was close,' whispered Gordon, alongside me.

'Too damn close for my liking,' said Bill. 'What the hell do we do now, go round?'

Scotty, who was lying on my other side, gave me a nudge and said, 'No, Basil, that's the way,' at the same time pointing down into the gorge. On looking down we could see that one side was in complete shade; fortunately it was the side nearest to us. We all looked at one another and nodded in agreement, so instead of backtracking and making a detour of many miles, we decided to trust our luck and go under the viaduct.

We waited until the German patrol had turned and gone up the track some distance, then silently, in single file, we made our way slowly along the floor of the gorge. Up above us we could hear the German guards calling back and forth across the viaduct, and all the while we were expecting to hear bullets come whistling in our direction.

Once clear of the immediate danger area, we stopped for a brief rest. We turned round, and looking up, we could clearly see the viaduct outlined against the moon. In the distance we heard a low rumbling noise, and after listening for a while, we realised that it was the sound of an approaching train. Sure enough, the train soon thundered on to the viaduct. Silhouetted against the moon we could see the engine, which was pulling a couple of carriages and behind them a great many table-top trucks carrying tanks, personnel carriers and guns. The train was heading east, so we assumed its destination was the Russian front; it would probably swing away to the north through Poland on a branch line to avoid the bombing of our planes, which we sometimes heard flying overhead on their night raids.

It was not long after this incident that we were confronted with a second obstacle in the form of a wide, swift-flowing river. Hoisting our packs on to one shoulder and holding them there with one arm, we linked hands to form a chain and waded in. To our relief the water came up only as high as our chests, and we were thus able to keep our packs dry.

Shortly afterwards, we came out of the forest onto what appeared to be the main highway running approximately north and south, so choosing the latter direction, we set off in single file, with big Scotty leading, and believe you me, when he was in front you knew you were moving.

I guess it must have been the glory of that wonderful moonlight night and the lovely aroma of the pines that lulled us into a false sense of security and made us careless. Here we were marching down the side of a white concrete road, which showed clearly in the bright moonlight, coming from somewhere and going to Lord knows where, disappearing into the distance as far as the eye could see.

We were totally unprepared for what happened next. Suddenly, silently, there appeared alongside us a German air force officer riding a bike. Going to the front of our column, he stopped and demanded, 'Halt! Wohin gehen Sie?' (Halt! Where are you going?) and his hand went towards the Luger pistol in the holster on his belt.

Now although taken by surprise, Scotty kept his cool and tried to explain to him, in bastard German, that we were on our way to an *Arbeitskommando*, or work camp, but we others noticed that all the time Scotty kept his fist closed and resting just above his hip, out of sight of the officer. He told us afterwards that had the German gone for his gun, he would have knocked him out. I didn't doubt that he would have done just that.

The officer listened in rapt attention to what Scotty was saying, and we could see by the puzzled look on his face that he probably only understood about half of what Scotty was trying to say to him. Then to our amazement and relief, he finally shrugged his shoulders, and getting on his bike, he peddled away down the road.

'Bloody hell, that was close. Good work, Scotty,' said Gordon.

'Aye mon,' said Scotty, 'a wee bitte, but I had yon mon covered,' and his accompanying grin made the rest of us feel that we had a cool and reliable bloke in our team.

'I'm glad it was you and not me. A great effort, Scotty,' I said.

'I'll second that,' said Bill. 'Now, let's get to hell out of here, before that officer tells anyone about seeing us, and sets the Gestapo on our trail.'

We lost no time in getting off that highway and swinging away to the south-east. We moved deeper into the pine forest, putting many miles between ourselves and our meeting with the German officer, until finally, absolutely exhausted, we dropped down on the pine needles. We decided not to trust our luck with any more incidents that night, and rolling up in our blankets, we fell sound asleep.

Now, before continuing this story, I must explain to you why, in all probability, that German officer believed our story of going to another work camp.

At that time, Germany had as slave labour upwards of ten million people from all over Europe. Many would go from job to job as directed, but to my knowledge they were generally accompanied by guards and were required to carry identification papers and show them on demand, either to the military or the Gestapo. Why that German officer did not ask for our papers remains a mystery to me to this day, for here we were, four men with packs on their backs, marching down a road at midnight.

What a time to be moving camp!

To be sure we were 'humping our blueys', but unlike that old-time swaggie who had no particular destination, we had a set course — south — and our clear goal was freedom. Sure, our packs were heavy, but our longing for freedom and fear of capture filled our thoughts every waking moment and helped us forget the weight on our backs.

The following two nights, we walked mile after mile through this beautiful land, the soft gentle light of the full moon lighting up crops of wheat, oats and ryegrass. During all this time, we did not see livestock of any description. We thought that maybe the Germans had taken them all to feed their armies, but later on we learnt that because of their small holdings, most of the Czech farmers kept the bulk of their livestock under cover, feeding them each morning and evening from the wonderful crops we had seen while walking through this fertile land.

We had another narrow escape on one of these nights, when all of a sudden, without warning, we walked into a German encampment which was well camouflaged under the thick canopy of pines. Before we realised it, we were right under the barrel of an ack-ack gun with machine-gun emplacements on either side of it, but whether the sentries were asleep, or had gone to wake up their relief, I don't know, because we were not challenged, and so made a hasty retreat.

On both these nights we camped in small clumps of pines, with the sound of running streams nearby; with the warmer weather, the conditions for sleeping out were ideal. We worked out our position to be somewhere to the north-east of Marienthal. At night we could hear the sound of heavy-calibre bombs being dropped on either that town or perhaps Olomouc, accompanied as usual by the noise of ack-ack shells exploding in the night sky.

An extraordinary thing happened to me the following night. It was tough going from the outset, steep hill after steep hill, and the visibility was poor in the thick pine forests. We thought that we must be on the border between Moravia and Slovakia. Suddenly, as we topped the rise, there before us was a beautiful open glade flooded with bright moonlight, and we were so taken by the beauty of this lovely scene that we stopped. No one said a word.

In the stillness of the night, there was not a sound. Inexplicably, I was overcome by a strange, uncanny feeling — it was quite eerie. I seemed to visualise, in this open glade, a scene from the distant past: horses tethered to trees, men and women standing around in groups talking and dressed in old-fashioned clothes of the last century — the women with long dresses and riding boots, the men with tight-fitting breeches and long riding boots reaching up to their knees. The scene had the appearance of a meeting place or assembly point for the beginning of a hunt.

This scenario (or figment of my imagination, as well you might call it) lasted but a fleeting moment and then was gone, but it left me with a deep feeling of loss, as though I had been part of that scene of long ago. I did not mention it to the boys, as they probably would have thought me nuts (and I wouldn't have blamed them), but to this day I can still visualise that scene in the forests of far-off Moravia.

We had now been travelling for eight nights, and although we estimated that we had travelled about 100 miles (160 km), to us it seemed more like 200, due, I guess, to the tension built up within ourselves, our narrow evasion of the not-too-friendly enemy, and the numerous detours we had to make to avoid being recaptured.

Remembering the note pinned on the door of our barracks just before our break-out, we had a strong feeling that if we were retaken, we would more than likely be shot, as at this stage of the war, with the invasion of Europe having just taken place, there were a lot of trigger-happy Gestapo on the loose.

On the ninth day, about two o'clock in the afternoon, we stood at the edge of the pine forest and looked out across the beautiful landscape shimmering in the bright sunlight, the fields of corn, wheat, barley and clover stretching away into the far distance. As we stood there, I think we all had the same idea: a walk in the daylight.

I broke the silence of our thoughts. 'What about it boys? Will we give it a try this afternoon?'

'I was thinking the same thing, Basil,' said Bill. 'Why not give it a go?'

'It's bloody risky, but I'm willing, what about you Scotty?' said Gordon.

'Lead on McDuff, and let's gang awa',' said Scotty with a grin.

We set off at a very smart pace in beautiful weather, but soon it began pouring with rain, and a series of mishaps dogged our footsteps. I would like to point out that at this stage, we viewed everyone with suspicion, not knowing whether they were friendly or otherwise, and so did our best to avoid making contact with anyone. As a result, we probably covered a lot more ground than we need have, as I'm sure most of the farmers and civilians we saw would have been only too glad to help us on our way.

First we came across two men loading a timber wagon, but with the mist and the rain, we managed to avoid them. Then crossing a small wheat field, we were observed by a farmer, who probably thought we were Germans. Not long after that incident, we were crossing a highway when Gordon, who was leading, found himself about ten yards from two German soldiers wheeling bikes, but keeping his cool, he led us nonchalantly past them whilst we followed behind, expecting to be challenged at any moment.

We decided not to trust our luck any further and camped in the woods for a couple of hours, waiting for the dark, feeling cold, wet and miserable, with our clothes sopping wet. About ten o'clock, we resumed our march over wild, hilly country. I suppose it was just as well it was rough going, as it helped to warm us up and raise our spirits, but by midnight we'd had enough, and easing our soaked packs to the ground, we lowered our aching bodies on to those wonderful pine needles, shed by the ever-protecting branches overhead, and went straightway to sleep.

6
Tondo

In this chapter, more so than in any other, I have had to rely mainly on my memory, as in all fairness to Tondo, a wonderful, hard-working man of the soil, my diary does not mention his name, or those of his companions, or the village where they lived.

Sure, I wrote in my diary every day during those weeks in which he hid and fed us, at the risk of being shot by the Gestapo. Such could also have been the fate of his companions, and most likely their homes would have been burnt to the ground. Right from that first meeting, and during the following weeks, all that was written in my diary was '9th Kip' (camp), '10th Kip,' 'still travelling,' and so on, and to this day, I cannot remember his surname, or the name of the village where he lived, and I doubt whether I could find it again, even if I travelled the same journey.

*   *   *

The next day, as if to make up for all our hardships, we walked through the beautiful, fertile land, with the sun shining down on us and crops stretching away on either side as far as the eye could see. This must surely be one of the most prolific food-growing areas of Europe; we wondered how much of the harvest went to feed Hitler's armies.

About five in the afternoon, while trying to avoid farmers working in the fields, we suddenly heard a whistle, and turning round, we saw a farmer walking towards us with a hoe over his shoulder. Taken somewhat by surprise, we watched his approach with apprehension, trying to sum up his attitude as he got nearer.

He was a man of average height, about five feet seven or eight, and dressed in the usual farmer's garb: long dark trousers, shirt with sleeves rolled up to the elbow, and the customary cap perched on his head. On reaching us, he lowered his hoe to the ground, and with an inquiring look and a sweeping gesture of his arm to include all of us, said what sounded like 'Nemetsky,' and seeing we did not understand, he made another attempt with the word 'Deutsch,' which we knew meant German. Hoping for the best, we gathered round him and replied, 'No, English'.

Well all our doubts vanished when we saw a warm friendly smile light up his face, and his exclamation, 'dobry, dobry,' reassured us and allayed our suspicions.

We tried to explain our different nationalities, but he shook his head and held up his hand, indicating that he wanted us to pay attention. A look of anxiety spread over his face as he gazed round in all directions, then beckoning us to follow, he led us into the middle of his wheat field and motioned us to get down in a shallow ditch. Then with a big grin and a nod of approval, he squatted down beside us, put his forefinger to his lips for silence, and with both hands extended, he made a sign for us to keep well down out of sight.

What followed was like pantomime sign language, except that we could see by the look on the farmer's face that he was in deadly earnest. First he pointed to the sun and swept his arm down the sun's path to the horizon; then holding both hands stretched towards us, with palms open and fingers fully extended, he lowered them to the ground. He then raised one hand with two fingers held up, and pointing to himself, blew three low whistles and indicated he would return. Finally, with a farewell wave, he shouldered his hoe and walked out of the wheat without looking back.

'Well, I don't know about you blokes,' said Gordon, 'but from what I could make out, that bloke reckons he'll be back here about 12 o'clock tonight.'

'Well,' I said, 'he seems a genuine bloke, and I'll bet he won't betray us'.

The other three were of the same opinion, so stretching out, we lay back and waited, but I know that in the back of all our minds we were wondered if we would be picked up by a German patrol or the Gestapo, or whether our new-found friend would prove to be just that and no more.

Lying there talking in whispers, and waiting anxiously while the sun gradually sank below the horizon, to be followed by the European twilight, I wondered about the preceding events and what the future held for us. Then the quietness of the night took over, and the big golden moon rose and shed its soft light over this beautiful but not so peaceful land.

Just as the moon was reaching its zenith, the stillness of the night was broken by three low soft whistles, and we waited somewhat anxiously, not knowing what to expect. Then a rustling of the wheat indicated the presence of someone close at hand, and suddenly our man appeared carrying a large jug, a big round loaf of bread and some cheese. Handing them to us, he pointed to his mouth.

'Gee, this is great! What a bloomin' treat. Thanks, mate,' said Bill, and we all joined in with our profuse thanks. We needed no second bidding to set to on the hot steaming coffee, delicious brown bread and home-made cheese.

Meanwhile, our friend was sitting a few yards away with a big grin on his face, obviously getting a lot of pleasure from our appreciation of his wonderful gifts. Any doubts that we may have had about our new friend were swept away, not only by his generous gift of food, but also by his forthright and friendly manner, and looking at him squatting there on his haunches, I knew that this was a person in whom one could have complete trust — a friend indeed.

When we had finished, he rose and beckoned us to follow, then led us across wheat and clover fields until finally we came to a halt in a shallow depression. There in front of us was what looked like a large two-man tent, about eight feet long and five feet high, but instead of canvas, the top and sides consisted of clover thrown over the wooden framework of a hay rack. On the ground inside were spread several large hessian bags.

Before motioning us inside, he pointed to himself and said 'Me Tondo'. So with grins all round, we introduced ourselves one by one, at the same time shaking his hand and telling him our different nationalities, and we all had a good laugh when he said with a grin on his face, 'League of Nations'. Then pointing to himself once again, and indicating with a sweep of his arm the eastern horizon, with the farewell words, 'dobrou noc,' and a wave of his hand, he strode away in the moonlight.

It was just on sunrise the following morning that we were awakened by what sounded like the words 'dobra itro,' repeated several times at the entrance to our new abode, and with bleary eyes we made out Tondo's smiling face. He had pulled aside the clover covering the opening of our sleeping quarters, and in his hands he held another large loaf of bread, some cheese, and a jug of coffee.

We crawled out and stood up to survey the surroundings of what was to be our home in the weeks ahead. On all sides were fields of wheat, clover and other crops such as sugar beet and potatoes, and not far away, on the edge of the wheat, was the pine forest which was to prove so very handy during our stay.

Thus began our association with this remarkable man Tondo, which was to develop into a strong friendship in the days ahead. We tried to thank him, and although there was a language barrier, he seemed to understand, nodding his head, and by different gestures indicated what we should do. First he pointed to the rising sun and swept his arm to the western horizon. Then pointing to all of us, he walked to the entrance of our shelter and indicated that we should go inside. We realised immediately that he wanted us to keep out of sight during the day, and we all nodded in agreement.

We thought that was the end of Tondo's request, but much to our amusement, with a grin on his face, he undid his belt and gave us a pretty good demonstration of going to the toilet, at the same time pointing at the sun then jabbing his finger several times towards the western horizon. Finally he gestured in the direction of the forest, and once again we understood that he wanted us to do our business in the forest, but only at night.

By now, we were becoming fairly proficient at interpreting Tondo's pantomime, so we nodded our assent and made a mental note to try and change Mother Nature's habits to suit the occasion. Tondo did up his belt, picked up the empty jug, and with a grin bade us 'dobrý den,' and trudged back to the village.

Thus was set the pattern for these early morning and evening visits, which we looked forward to with great pleasure. I can say without any doubt that the days and weeks that followed were some of the most pleasant and enjoyable of our whole trip.

That evening, just after sundown, we four were sitting just inside the entrance to our clover shelter, playing euchre with a pack of cards we'd brought with us. The twilight was just starting to fade when Tondo arrived with the usual delightful meal of bread, cheese and coffee, but this time he was accompanied by a tall, distinguished-looking stranger, probably in his early forties.

Tondo introduced us, and to our surprise, the man addressed us in very good English. 'Good evening gentlemen,' he said, adding with a chuckle, 'Tondo tells me that you are the League of Nations. That is good; we will sit down round the table and have a little debate.' He pointed to the ground outside the entrance to our shelter, and as we squatted in a circle, he proceeded to tell us a most sorrowful tale of the happenings in his country since the German occupation.

'Firstly,' he said, 'I must tell you my name, which is Tondo, the same as my good friend here, and stands for Tony or Anthony in your language. I was a professor at the University of Prague until the Germans closed it down, and I am now manager of the cheese factory in the nearby village.'

I looked across at Tondo, who nodded his head. There was a look of admiration as he glanced at the Professor, and I knew there was a strong bond of friendship between these two men.

The Professor continued. 'My main purpose, aside from wanting to meet all of you, was to warn you of the danger you are in from the Gestapo, who are right throughout Czechoslovakia. Have you ever heard of the village of Lidice?'

We shook our heads, and he went on with his narrative, but his voice had a hard timbre to it and we could feel the underlying hatred as he poured out this gruesome story:

'Well, maybe you have heard of Heydrich, 'the Butcher of Prague,' Hitler's *Reichsprotektor* of Bohemia and Moravia, head of the Gestapo, and responsible for the liquidation of the Jews. A truly fiendish and cruel bastard of a man, who used to sit at the window of his home, Castle Hradčany in Prague, and watch the execution of Czech citizens, who were put against a wall in the courtyard below and shot.

'Hitler and this butcher Heydrich had between them established a policy, or should I say a brutal line of action, that went by the name of *Nacht und Nebel* (night and fog). In practice, this sinister phrase meant simply 'extermination' of anyone opposing German rule in the conquered countries, particularly the Jews. Now if I am boring you, please stop me, as I am really wound up tonight.'

We all shook our heads, as by this time he had us well and truly interested in this sordid but fascinating tale, which sounded almost unbelievable, more like fiction than fact.

'Well, the intelligence service in England, and Churchill himself, had heard of Heydrich's barbaric atrocities, and it was decided to assassinate him. So four Czechs were chosen from a number of volunteers and sent to a training camp near the Canada-U.S. border,* where they were taught the art of underground guerrilla warfare. They were then flown to Czechoslovakia and dropped by parachute in the countryside near Prague.

'On May 27th, 1942, the men ambushed Heydrich's car a few miles outside Prague and killed him with a hand grenade. The reprisals were horrific. Hitler, in all his madness and fury, ordered 10 000 Czech hostages taken, and 100 a day were executed.' The Professor paused, and we began to realise under what terrific strain these Czechs were living.

'Now this is where I come to the part of my story about the village of Lidice,' said the Professor. 'The village was not far from the assassination point, and Hitler vented his wrath on it. Every man, woman and child in

---

* This may well have been Camp X, the top-secret training camp run by the British in southern Ontario, Canada. However, other sources suggest that the parachutists were trained in the UK. (Ed.)

that village was either shot, burnt to death in a big barn, or sent to the gas chambers of Ravenstock. Finally, Lidice was burnt to the ground with flame-throwers.'

We sat silent for a moment, stunned by the enormity of this horrible massacre of innocent men, women and children. Then gradually it dawned on us, what it was the Professor was trying to convey to us in recounting this graphic story. We now realised fully the danger we were in, not only that, but the fact that by our very presence, we were endangering the lives of these two wonderful people, and indeed of the whole village. I looked at my companions and could see the looks of concern on their faces. I knew they grasped the situation, and I spoke up:

'Listen, Professor and Tondo, what you have told us has only just now made the four of us realise the danger in which we have placed you and your people in the village. I think we should pack up and move on this very night, and I guess my companions feel the same way.' There was an instant reply from the boys, who spoke and nodded their complete agreement.

The Professor held up both hands for silence. 'Now, don't be too hasty Basil,' he said. 'All I was trying to convey to you was the seriousness of the situation in which you are placed — and also my friends over there,' pointing in the direction of the village.

He went on, 'You must understand that we Czechs are not fools. We have an underground organisation every bit as good as, if not better than the Gestapo. Every move they make is watched day and night, and warnings go out well ahead of their evil intentions. Please stay awhile. I can assure you that you and my people are quite safe, providing that you do what we tell you and keep out of sight.'

I looked at my three mates and said, 'What do you think boys?'

We went into a huddle, discussing the pros and cons of the situation, and eventually and quite reluctantly agreed to stay a little longer, at the same time extracting a promise from the Professor that he was to tell us immediately if we were in any way putting anyone's life in danger. He and Tondo stayed and chatted a while, then getting to their feet they bade us 'dobrou noc', which we guessed was good night, and with a cheery wave walked off into the night.

The following evening, Tondo arrived with the usual gift of nourishing food, but this time he also brought a scribbling pad and pencil. Pointing to me, he held up the pad, and flourishing the pencil, he said 'English,' then pointing to himself, he said 'Czech,' and made to write a word on the pad. So began our gesticulating sign language, and to this day I can still remember the two of us sitting there in those long twilight evenings, and our first lesson, when he pointed to the loaf of bread and said what sounded like 'klep,' so I wrote down in my diary 'bread,' pronouncing it very slowly, and Tondo copied it down on his pad and opposite it he wrote the word 'chleb,' which I also copied into my diary.

I guess that what Tondo and I were doing at that moment had been done many times before by those early explorers and intrepid adventurers (Marco Polo, David Livingstone, and many others) into Arabic lands and further afield, where the classroom was in very strange surroundings, and where the teachers were also pupils at one and the same time.

We started on the articles of food, and then proceeded to name the parts of the body, starting at the head, and when we got below the belt, Tondo pointed to my privates with a grin, at which we all had a good laugh, such was his earthy humour, which we were to know only too well in the coming weeks.

When we had finished with our clothing, Tondo held up his hand, saying 'dost,' which I guessed meant enough or finish. As he got to his feet and put pencil and pad in his pocket, he pointed to the east, saying 'zítra,' which I thought must mean tomorrow, and bidding us all 'dobrou noc,' he strode away into the darkness.

'We needna worry aboot yon mon,' said Scotty.

'I'll second that,' said Bill.

'I don't think we need worry about the Gestapo with those two watchdogs around,' said Gordon.

'I think we can sleep soundly at night,' I said. 'It seems we have arrived at the right place, with truly wonderful people.'

Tondo arrived very early the next morning, just on dawn, and greeting us with his usual remark, 'dobré jitro,' he gave us our breakfast. Then squatting down alongside me, he pulled out pencil and pad, and looking at him, I could see by the eager look on his face how keen he was to begin the day's lesson. He repeated his early morning greeting and wrote in his pad, 'dobré jitro'.

'I guess he means 'good morning,'' I said to the boys, and wrote the English translation for him on his pad and the Czech words in my diary. Then we went on to the words 'dobrý den' (good day), 'dobrý večer' (good evening), 'dobrou noc' (good night), with all the accompanying waving of arms and pointing to the different positions of the sun in the sky. Tondo was an avid learner, and his quick, keen understanding of what our English words meant amazed all of us. I had always had a liking for different languages and tried hard to master the meaning of those difficult Slavonic words and verbs. We both did our best to try to pronounce and comprehend each other's translations.

The lesson finished, Scotty (who didn't say much, but when he did it generally made good sense) spoke up. 'Tondo,' he said, 'we canna be takin' a' of ye food wi'out gi'n ye some of our own,' and with that he reached into our shelter and pulled his pack out, and from it took some of the remaining tins of food.

We three nodded our assent and rummaged in our packs also, taking out small tins of bully and what remained of our biscuits and milk. We offered these to Tondo, but he held up his hands in protest and shook his head vigorously. We could see by the determination written on his face that he was not going to accept the articles of food we wanted to give him, but finally we persuaded him to take our packets of tea, as he understood quite clearly that we could not light a fire. The pleasure we got in seeing his face light up, and his words, 'díky, díky,' which we guessed must have been a form of thanks, gave us a good deal of satisfaction in being able to repay him in some form for his kindness.

These early morning and evening visits were to become the routine of our daily lives in the weeks ahead. Each morning we would see men and women, with scythes or hoes over their shoulders, coming from the village and making their way to the plots, which radiated out from the village like the spokes of a wheel. There they would spend the whole day chipping weeds in the corn or sugar beet, or cutting clover and throwing it over the long wooden racks that dotted the landscape. In the evenings, they would collect the dried clover from these same racks and pile it on long V-shaped wooden carts, which were generally pulled by cows or oxen. For everyone, then, the day's work was at an end, and shouldering hoes and scythes they would follow the carts back to the village for a well-earned rest.

This method of farming had probably been going on from generation to generation, and the beauty, tranquillity and serenity of this peaceful country scene were not lost on me; they recalled the lines of that wonderful piece of work by Thomas Gray, *Elegy Written in a Country Church-Yard*:

> *The curfew tolls the knell of parting day,*
> *The lowing herd wind slowly o'er the lea,*
> *The plowman homeward plods his weary way,*
> *And leaves the world to darkness and to me.*
>
> *Now fades the glimmering landscape on the sight,*
> *And all the air a solemn stillness holds,*

Save where the beetle wheels his droning flight,
And drowsy tinklings lull the distant folds …

The whole village knew we were there, and on several occasions, Tondo brought some of his men friends down at night and jokingly introduced us as his 'League of Nations' friends. We soon found out that they were all part of the Czech underground movement; we knew only too well the risk they were taking and what would happen to them if the Gestapo caught them harbouring some escaped POWs.

So for their sakes especially, we kept a very low profile. Any exercise we had was done at night, with short walks through the crops and into the forest to attend to Mother Nature's demands. During the day we spent many hours playing poker, rummy, euchre and five hundred, or else just lying around sleeping and looking forward to the end of the day, when we could stretch our legs.

It was during this period of inactivity, while we were cooped up in such a small space during the long hot summer days, that the first signs of dissension began to appear — petty squabbles and small disagreements over the cards and various other small incidents that were accentuated and enlarged mainly, I think, as a result of our confined space. As time went by, the arguments and rows became more intense and personal. Bill and I, the two Aussies, stuck together; Gordon and Scotty also paired up in these verbal clashes.

I could see what might happen if this situation were to continue. We could come to blows. I was worried for the success of our venture.

One morning, out of the blue, Scotty said, 'I think I'll gang awa'. I canna bide here any mere.'

'I'm with you, Scotty. Neither can I,' said Gordon.

I looked at Bill, who said, 'Hang on, you blokes, I know we've had some bloody arguments, but what the hell, it's only because these cramped conditions have stirred us all up. Let's stay a little longer and save up some of the tucker that Tondo's giving us. We haven't much food left.'

'That sounds sensible enough,' I said. 'After all, we have a damn long way to go to reach our destination.' So we all agreed to stay a while longer and save up some rations.

As if in answer to our problems, one evening, just after dark, we heard the usual three whistles and could make out Tondo's form as he approached. As he got nearer, however, we noticed a large sack over his shoulder, and dumping the sack on the ground, he produced shirts, trousers, coats and caps, and handed each of us a complete set of clothes according to our size. He did not stay long. After indicating that we should wear these clothes, he bade us 'dobrou noc,' and with our profuse thanks ringing in his ears, he waved us goodbye and strode away into the darkness.

'Well I'll be damned,' said Bill. 'What do you make of this?'

'I think it's a bloody good idea,' said Gordon. 'Makes us one of them, and less likely to be noticed by the Gestapo.'

'I wonder if they're going to let us work in the fields with them,' I said.

'By cripes Basil, I hope to hell you're right,' said Bill, and our spirits rose with the thought that we'd able to leave our confined quarters during the heat of the day.

When Tondo arrived next morning, we were all dressed in our new outfits, which were very similar to those worn by the local farmers, though mine seemed to be somewhat newer. On seeing us, Tondo threw up his hands, exclaiming 'dobrý, dobrý,' and pointing at the others, said slowly, in very broken English, 'You three farmers'. Then pointing at me, he added, 'You one English gentleman'.

We all roared with laughter, and pointing to myself, I said, 'Me boss. Me no work,' which he seemed to understand, as he nodded with that ever-ready grin.

That evening, Tondo arrived with the Professor, who shook hands with us all, saying, 'Good evening gentlemen, I trust you slept well?'

'With you two blokes around, I don't think we need worry very much,' said Gordon.

'You have an abiding faith in our ability,' said the Professor.

'Well,' I said, 'if anything was going to happen to us, I think the spooks would have come in the night and spirited us away long before now.'

The Professor threw back his head and laughed, but not too loudly, and when he translated to Tondo what I had said, he also went into fits of laughter; the boys, of course, joined in the merriment.

The Professor held up his hand. 'We make just a little too much noise,' he said. 'Would you please follow us. Tondo and I have a little surprise for you.'

So with wonder and curiosity, we fell into line behind them and walked silently through the night, having been cautioned by the Professor not to make a sound. On the outskirts of the village we came to a large square concrete building, and after making our way round to the back, the Professor produced a key from his pocket, opened a fairly solid door and ushered us into a long hallway. With Tondo bringing up the rear, we filed in and followed the Professor down the corridor until he held up his hand as a signal to stop. Then turning the handle of another door, the Professor beckoned us into what seemed, by the light of his torch, to be a fairly large room. When we had all crowded in, Tondo shut the door behind us and switched on the light.

We could see at a glance that it was an office of some kind. There was a large desk, on top of which were a typewriter and papers in wire baskets; against one wall were some iron cupboards. Over the window, for safety's sake, were draped several layers of very thick curtains. What caught our eye, however, was a small table carrying several large bottles of what appeared to be wine, some glasses, and plates laden with cakes and slices of bread and cheese.

The Professor, noticing the direction of our glances, walked over to the table, uncorked some bottles, and handing round the glasses, said, 'Help yourselves, boys, to some plum brandy, or should I say, 'Get stuck into it?" And thus started off an evening I was never to forget.

You know, I have always had the idea that life is mainly a series of experiences, and the more you have, the richer and more fulfilling is the reward, providing, I suppose, that the good have somewhat outnumbered the bad. This occasion was one of those rare, once only, very good experiences, shared with comradely *joie de vivre* by a group of men of mixed nationalities, under circumstances that were spiced with a little excitement and danger.

During the course of the evening, as the brandy flowed, so did our confidence and friendship increase. Tondo and our new friend the Professor were obviously enjoying our company and were chatting away merrily, Tondo doing his best to understand what was being said. I could not help noticing that any estrangement between the four of us had melted away in the enjoyment of this unusual party.

When the Professor held up his hand for silence, the conversation died down, and seating ourselves on the floor, with our backs against the walls, we listened as he went on to say, with a quiet voice tinged with a little sadness and bitterness:

'I will tell you something of the recent history of this wonderful land of ours, now suffering under the heel of the German jackboot. You have probably heard of the 1938 Munich Agreement, which gave Hitler a starting point for his annexation of the Sudetenland,* followed by the full-scale invasion of Bohemia and Moravia.'

---

* The Sudetenland almost enclosed the Czech (western) part of the country, and had a large population of Germans.

He told us of the heartbreak and despair of the soldiers of the once-powerful Czechoslovakian army, which was so well trained and equipped as to be one of the strongest in Europe, and he tried to convey to us the anger and bitterness these soldiers felt when told to lay down their arms, realising that no help was forthcoming from England, France or Russia.

'Czechoslovakia,' he said, 'gained independence in 1918. When the Franco-Czech-Soviet alliance became a thing of the past, the rot set in, and the German-Soviet non-aggression pact, signed in August 1939, sealed the fate, not only of Poland, but also indirectly, in the long run, of France and the whole of Europe.'

Their once proud and democratic country was now ruled with an iron hand by the Third Reich. Himmler's brutal SS troops and the dreaded Gestapo were in full control. When the Germans annexed their country, Hitler dictated that Bohemia and Moravia were to become a protectorate, or in other words, to be incorporated into the Third Reich. Slovakia, the eastern half of the country, spent most of the war as a puppet state of the Reich under a government led by Father Josef Tiso. It, too, lost much of its territory, in this case mostly to Hungary.

The Germans took over everything, including a vast amount of war materials and factories associated with the making of arms. All surplus grain and other foodstuffs were railed back to Germany, and Germans were put in charge of industry and banking. The regional districts of Bohemia and Moravia, and for that matter the politics of the whole country, were completely run by Germany. The University of Prague, where the Professor had taught, was closed, as were all Czech colleges, and riots broke out in the streets of Prague, where a student was shot by the German police. Brutal reprisals followed. SS troops shot quite a number of students and took thousands more away to Buchenwald concentration camp for torture and death.

'Come,' he said. 'I grow too morbid. Drink up and we will have a little music.' Going to the cabinets standing against the wall, he took out a mandolin, and patting it with his hand, he said, 'One of my little amusements. I will now sing for you a beautiful Czech song about this wonderful land of ours.'

He had a magnificent voice. We sat enthralled by his rich, melodious tones, sung with deep feeling and tinged with sadness. Listening to this beautiful song, memories of the past, of those wonderful times I had in the pre-war years, came flooding back, seeming to appear as a clear picture. A great longing to be home with my loved ones took possession of my whole being.

Looking at my three mates, I wondered if they had the same feelings. On Tondo's face was a look of intense rapture and there was a touch of moisture in his eyes. Perhaps he too was thinking of those peaceful pre-war days, and of the young men and women sent away to concentration camps or to labour as slaves in the factories of Hitler's war machine.

The Professor insisted that we sing an Australian song, so we gave a hearty rendition of 'Waltzing Matilda,' and just as Gordon was about to sing 'The Maori's Farewell', there was a knock at the door. A man hurried in, put his finger to his lips, and his one word — 'Shush!' — was full of meaning. Then after speaking a few quiet words to Tondo and the Professor, he left the room, closing the door quietly behind him.

'We make too much noise,' said the Professor. 'I think perhaps we should be a little quieter; the plum brandy seems to be having quite a good effect.' There was a good-humoured grin on his face.

His words had a sobering effect, making us realise what silly asses we were, and reminding us of the danger in which we were placing our friends and of the fact that we were being protected by the partisans, who were keeping a sharp watch outside. The evening ended on a more subdued and maudlin note, for we consumed numerous bottles of the potent brandy, staggering to our bunks in the early hours of the morning.

Oh boy, what a hangover! When Tondo arrived just on sunrise, looking as bright as a button, he found us groaning and holding our heads, all thoughts of departure forgotten.

'What did ye gi'e us in yon bottles, mon?' asked Scotty with a groan.

'Dobra den,' said Tondo with a big grin, waving at the sky.

'Like bloody hell it is,' said Gordon.

Tondo shook his head in sympathy, but then, with a sweep of his arm, he pointed in the direction of the wheat, which was ripening in the fields. Next, he walked over to us and seemed to compare what he was wearing with what we had on. Finally, with both arms, he gave a good demonstration of using a scythe.

Bill of course, being a farmer, was the first to grasp the meaning of this pantomime. 'He needs a hand with the harvest,' he said.

We all readily agreed, glad of the opportunity to get away from the boredom and cramped quarters of our clover shelter. Tondo left us with our early morning meal, indicating that he'd return later, and with a cheery wave and a big grin, held his head between his hands, shook his head sadly, and walked back to the village.

'What a great bloke and what a godsend to have a friend like that. He's one in a million,' I said.

How the atmosphere had changed! Here we were sitting round chatting amiably, whereas before we would hardly have spoken to one another. What a difference Tondo's kind words and actions had made to our feelings towards one another — a true friend if ever there was one.

It was really something to see the men, with long-handled scythes over their shoulders, followed by the women, in long dresses and with scarves over their hair, walking out to the fields to begin the day's harvest. I guess this was the pattern of their lives, down through the years.

Watching this scene, my thoughts went back to those hot summer days in the wheat fields outside Inverell, to my old Dad, sitting atop his Sunshine Harvester, driving his team of six powerful Clydesdales, which would strain in the harness, pulling that machine from early morning to dusk, yet seeming to enjoy every minute of their hard task. At the end of the day was their frisky gallop down to the waters of the Macintyre River to wade and drink their fill.

Tondo, who was leading the group out of the village, beckoned us over. We could see that he had two scythes, one of which he gave to Bill, saying, 'Me think you good farmer', and much to our wonder, his judgement was spot on.

Now these scythes differed slightly from the ordinary run-of-the-mill ones, for near the end of the blade was attached a long piece of cane, which extended in a curve like a bow to about 18 inches up the handle, where it was fastened securely.

To watch Tondo swing his scythe hour after hour, was a pleasure to behold; he seemed absolutely tireless. With rhythmic stroke he collected a considerable bunch of stalks, which in turn were gathered into bundles and tied up by the women following behind.

Looking around in every direction, we could see men and women performing the same tasks. With each swishing stroke, the golden heads of wheat fell with unerring accuracy, while the womenfolk kept pace all through the day. Their forefathers must have displayed the same consummate skill, which had been handed down the line till it came to a son like Tondo, of whom they would have been proud.

We four tried our hand with the scythe, much to Tondo's amusement, but Bill was the only one who could mange the rhythmic stroke, so he fell in behind Tondo and started to cut the next swath. The rest of us followed, tying the wheat into sheaves with a couple of strands of stalk and standing them in stooks on the field.

The women worked alongside us in the next patch, bending to their task and chatting amongst themselves. Every once in a while they would give us a shy glance, the younger ones probably thinking about which one of us they would like to have in their beds for the night. And so through the long summer days, working side by side, we established a strong camaraderie, engendered by the common enemy occupying the country.

How we used to enjoy the morning and afternoon coffee breaks, when down from the village would come two women carrying large jugs of coffee, loaves of bread, *maslo* (butter) and fish paste. We would sit around in a circle, with much laughter and giggling on the part of the women, and I can tell you it was like the Mad Hatter's tea party in *Alice in Wonderland* as we tried to understand one another's language. Sitting there, acting as master of ceremonies, was Tondo, who was thoroughly enjoying every minute of this bizarre gathering.

We didn't go back to the village for lunch, as it would have endangered the lives of these wonderful people, but instead returned to our hay-rack shelter. Tondo would bring us a lunch of vermicelli and vegetable soup, and knedlíky (dumplings) with sugar syrup or apricot jam, which were excellent.

Through all these long working days, during morning and afternoon tea breaks — sorry, I should say coffee breaks — and even while we were at lunch, we would look around, and in the distance we could see a man watching us from just outside the village, or at the edge of the forest. Tondo, when questioned, would point to his eyes and say, 'Gestapo'. Well, enough said, we knew we had friends keeping watch.

One day, shortly after the harvest had begun, we were joined at our morning coffee break by the Professor, and during a lull in the conversation, the topic of our destination was brought up. With a touch of concern in his voice, he said, 'Please, you four, I would be very interested to know where you intend to go from this place.'

I replied, 'We are going home for Xmas'.

Well, he roared with laughter, and when he told the others what I had said, there were grins and more laughter round the circle of these friendly folk. His 'I wish you all a Merry Xmas, and God speed,' was said with all sincerity, and it gave us a feeling of warm friendship towards them all.

*   *   *

The harvest was finished, and the carts had carried the stooks from the fields. A few days later, it began to drizzle, and by evening it was steadily getting worse. Not long after dark, Tondo appeared on the scene, and putting a finger to his lips to keep silent, he indicated that we should collect our belongings and follow him. So picking up our packs, we trailed along in single file, just barely able to make out his figure in the darkness, and eventually came to a large barn on the outskirts of the village. We entered the barn by the back door, which Tondo hurriedly shut after us. He then struck a match and lit what looked like a hurricane lamp. Holding it up, he walked over to a ladder leaning against a wooden rail above our heads, and beckoning us over, he pointed towards the top of the ladder. Climbing up, we found ourselves in a large hay loft, and with Tondo's warning 'shush' and 'dobrou noc' ringing in our ears, we settled down on the strong-smelling, wonderfully warm, newly cut hay, and fell sound asleep.

The sound of Tondo's 'dobré jitro, káva' woke us in the early morning, and we opened our eyes to see him standing not far from the top of the ladder, with the usual jug of coffee in one hand and a big round loaf of bread and some cheese in the other. With a cheery grin, he said in halting English, 'Breakfast ready, sir,' a wonderful, reassuring way to be woken in such strange surroundings. We all had a good laugh, giving him our good mornings and thanks as the rain poured down outside, and we stretched ourselves and sat up to face a new day.

Taking stock of our surroundings, we noticed that the hay loft ran right round the top of the barn, and from where we were, we looked down on to a wide open space surrounded by cattle pens. Soon all was activity. Tondo began throwing hay down to the women below, and while some of them fed the cattle, others began the day's milking; the zinging sound as streams of milk hit the bottom of the pails soon reached our ears.

This was the usual routine in the days to follow. It rained without ceasing, and we mostly passed the time away playing cards, sleeping, lazing about, and trying to improve the language situation with Tondo.

One morning, just after milking, our routine was broken. We heard someone climbing a ladder, and waiting expectantly, we saw the head and shoulders of a rather pretty girl come into view over the edge of the loft. With a sweet smile, she greeted us with the usual 'dobré jitro,' climbed up into the loft, and came and sat down alongside us. There was much gesticulating and laughter, and of course one or two of the boys started to get fresh with this vivacious piece of femininity, but their advances were playfully rebuffed. I guess it was only our numbers that prevented her from being tumbled, as I think the boys would have had a willing and enthusiastic partner.

But that was not our only visitor. Sometimes of an early morning, Tondo would come hurrying in, and climbing the ladder, would motion us, with a warning 'shush,' to lie down flat, then quickly cover us with hay and nonchalantly start pitch-forking some of it down to the women below. The word Gestapo carried a lot of menace.

One particular morning, we could hear the sound of guttural voices down below, questioning the women as they milked and went about their usual chores. 'Was ist oben?' (What is above?) we could hear one German say in a loud voice to Tondo, and Tondo's reply — 'Nur Heu' (only hay) — was said in a most casual manner as he went on pitching hay down to the women below.

The German climbed the ladder and poked his head over the edge of the loft, whilst Tondo's fork went perilously close to giving us a jab. With a grunt, and apparently satisfied, the German retreated down the ladder and rejoined his companion, and together they left the barn. It was Tondo's warning 'shush,' once again, that made us lie perfectly still for quite some time before he gave us the all-clear.

'Phew, that was bloody close,' said Gordon, sitting up and brushing the hay off himself.

'What you mean, or should I say what we mean is, 'Good on you Tondo,'' I said with feeling in my voice, and the others chimed in with hearty thanks. We all knew the great risk he had taken, probably saving our lives at the risk of his own.

*   *   *

The rain stopped. We returned to our bivouac, and it wasn't long before we were squabbling amongst ourselves once again. A restlessness set in, and now that the harvest was finished, we decided that we must continue our journey; we had a long way to go before we reached Yugoslavia and only two or three months before the cold of a European winter set in, which would make travelling impossible.

And so in the gathering dusk, a small group of men stood in a circle just inside the edge of the forest. Farewells come in many ways, but this one had a certain sadness and finality about it. We four knew in our own hearts that we would probably never see Tondo or the Professor again. I can still see Tondo standing there with a grin on his face, moisture in his eyes. He pointed at me and said, 'You going home for Xmas.'

We swung away to the south through the pines. Then we turned briefly to wave to those two wonderful people, Tondo and the Professor. They stood there with arms upraised, giving us the V for victory sign. The memory of that parting is with me to this day.

7

Ever Onward

We strode silently through the pines in single file, reminding me of those James Fenimore Cooper yarns about American Indians on the warpath. Sure, there was a war going on, but we were the hunted, not the hunters, and the paths we trod would be tricky ones. We did not delude ourselves for one moment about the dangers that lay ahead. Yugoslavia was a long way away.

Each of our packs now contained a large, round loaf and big hunks of cheese, farewell gifts from Tondo and the Professor, but of our own rations, all we had left was some of the oatmeal cake, which we had kept as a last resort. So with packs considerably lighter than when we had started, we headed southwards, but after a few hours decided to camp for the night and continue our walk the next day.

In the morning, we came across two old men picking mushrooms; they were whistling at intervals so they wouldn't lose sight of one another in the dense forest. Then we met up with a young man, a Czech, who had been working in various factories in Germany. The Gestapo found out that he had Jewish blood in his family, or so they said, and put him on a train bound for the death camps in Poland, but he had managed to jump from the train and escape into the forest. He seemed a very talented young man. He told us, in very good English, that he spoke five languages, one of which was Chinese, which he had learned while living in China with his father, a Czech diplomat.

During these days of marching, we saw hundreds of Allied bombers on their way to targets in Germany; we could only guess that they must have come up from bases in Italy. How small and terribly insignificant they made us feel, like ants crawling over unfamiliar territory. But like ants, we, too, had an intense homing instinct, and even though we were four lonely figures in a far-away land, surrounded by warring nations, we had a strong feeling that one day we would reach our destination.

After almost a week of travel, we consulted our map and worked out our position to be somewhere near St. Hostyns, and thus still a fair way from the Hungarian border. On this particular day, after climbing a steep rise, we came to a clearing in the pines, in the middle of which was a high steel structure, either a trig point or a fire lookout station. We decided to climb to the top of this tower to get a bearing on our direction and to spy out the land that lay ahead.

What a magnificent view — pine forests and farmlands stretching away to the south, and down below us a beautiful stream meandering through the trees and out across the tilled lands beyond. We decided to rest for a few days, so chose a well-concealed spot in the pines, alongside a beautiful pool. After taking off our packs, the first thing we did was to divest ourselves of our smelly clothes and dive starkers into the breathtakingly cold water.

So far the tides of fortune were running our way and my prayers had been answered. Someone up there must surely have liked us and guided our footsteps under a mantle of safety to this sheltered haven in the pines.

We had now exhausted our food supply and we roamed far and wide into the nearby fields, for safety's sake mainly at twilight and in the gathering dusk. Each of us brought back to camp the spoils of his search — sugar beet, corn and potatoes for the most part, the last of which we obtained by bandicooting (removing potatoes from below the surface of the ground, but leaving the top of the plant intact), reminding me very much of the film *All Quiet on the Western Front*. We also picked a lot of raspberries, which were growing in profusion in the forest. Amazing, isn't it, how quickly the human body adapts to different foods? We were now down to the basic fundamentals, complete vegetarians, all of us in splendid good health — not even a cold — and our bodies strong and tough.

During our stay in this idyllic place, there was another of those incidents that stand out so vividly in my mind and portray the sterling qualities of the people of this beleaguered land.

We came across an elderly, grey-haired, aristocratic-looking man who was wandering through the forest picking mushrooms. On our approach, he greeted us with the usual 'dobrý den,' and continued talking to us in the same language, to which we replied by shaking our heads, indicating that we did not understand, and asked him did he speak English? He shook his head, and we tried him with 'Sprechen Sie Deutsch?' (Do you speak German). 'Ah ja,' he replied, but his 'Was spricht deine Mutter?' left us a little puzzled until I realised that 'What speaks your mother?' must mean 'What is your nationality?'

'Wir sind Australisch' (We are Australian), I replied.

'Gut, sehr gut' (good, very good), he answered, and after that we managed to communicate rather slowly, getting on very well with the old chap. When we parted, he said, 'Morgen, ich wieder komme. Bleiben Sie hier' (In the morning, I will return. Wait here), and with that he turned, waved, and walked away through the forest.

The next day we waited just inside the timber line, and as the morning wore on, we decided that something must have prevented him from coming. Towards midday, however, we sighted our friend of the previous day strolling down the strip of land which divided the forest from the fields. Accompanying him was a beautiful girl wheeling a large pram, and although they saw us standing in the shadows, they walked right on by for about another hundred yards, then turned casually into the forest. The old chap was bending over with a basket in one hand, ostensibly looking for mushrooms, and when they had reached a fairly thick part of the forest, they stopped, and looking round to make sure that no one else was in the vicinity, beckoned us over. We walked over slowly to join them, whereupon the old chap introduced us to this lovely girl: 'Dies ist meine Tochter Hilga' (This is my daughter Hilga). Her 'Guten Tag' (good day), accompanied by an attractive smile, put us at our ease.

Without more ado, the old chap threw back a quilt, and our eyes fairly goggled. The pram was full of food — tomatoes, cobs of corn, cheese, small cakes and four loaves of bread. We unloaded the pram, quite overwhelmed with their generosity, but they brushed aside our thanks and said they must go back; their mention of the Gestapo made us realise they were risking their lives for us. We told them that on no account must they return, but they said they would try to get back in a few days, and before they left, the old chap warned us of German patrols in the area.

And so these two wonderful people left us, wheeling out of the forest and out of our lives, for after three days, when they did not return, we broke camp and hit the trail south, hoping and praying that no harm would come to such splendid people.

*   *   *

The strain of the journey was beginning to have an effect on all of us. Every waking hour was one of extreme watchfulness; every person we saw a potential Gestapo agent. I'm sure this is why once again we started to argue amongst ourselves, and as before, over the smallest of incidents, with Scotty and Gordon taking sides against Bill and me.

It was not only these stupid, trivial disagreements that made us decide to split up. It was also the nature of the country, which was becoming more open, with much bigger farms interspersed with high ridges covered with thick pine forests. There were also many more people about, and with four of us, we were likely to attract attention. We thus made up our minds to part company.

Slowly and reluctantly we packed our gear, dragging out our movements to prolong the time of departure. We stood, Bill and I on one side, and Gordon and Scotty about an arm's length away on the other. For a while no one said a word. I know that in my throat was a fair-sized lump, which momentarily made me unable to speak, and I'm sure the others felt the same way.

It was Gordon who first broke the silence with 'Good luck, you blokes'.

'And the same to you,' said Bill quietly.

'We're all going home for Xmas,' I said, trying to raise a grin.

'Aye mon, that we are, and guid luck to ye both.' Scotty's parting words were 'Lang may your rum reek,' which I found out later means 'Long may your chimney smoke'. What a sincere farewell from the usually quiet Scotsman.

We finally shook hands all round, wished each other a safe journey and God speed, and shouldering our packs, we waved farewell. Gordon and Scotty were heading east to try to contact the Russian forces, whilst Bill and I had decided to cross Hungary and join up with Tito's partisans in Yugoslavia.

Bill and I didn't go very far, staying in the area for nearly a week, bandicooting more spuds and gathering as much food as it was possible to carry, for we knew that the next stage of our march was going to be a tough one. To cross Hungary we would have to do all our walking at night, since the Hungarians were fighting on the side of the Germans and would not take too kindly to enemy aliens wandering around their country.

*   *   *

On August 20th, nearly two months on the run, we finally left the area and straight away ran into a spot of trouble. The going was fairly easy the first day, but while walking through a pine forest, Bill and I noticed a small cottage made of logs. What aroused our curiosity was the fact that it appeared to be newly constructed, with a fresh coat of paint, and somehow instinct told us to give it a wide berth, which we did. We followed a path through the trees and were crossing a large field of clover, which had recently been cut, when all of a sudden Bill grabbed me and pulled me down behind the windrow of hay.

I wondered what the hell was going on, but peering through the straw in the direction of Bill's intent gaze, I immediately realised what his swift action was all about. Coming down the path we'd just left, and not far away, were two German soldiers with rifles over their shoulders; they were scanning the fields in every direction. We lay there not daring to move a muscle, but what made it worse was the fact that we had to gone to ground on an ants' nest, and the insects immediately began crawling up our trouser legs and nipping our delicacies.

Finally the two soldiers gave up their search and walked back up the track, but with finger to his lips, Bill motioned me to lie still, and we remained in this position for at least another half hour while the ants continued to enjoy their lunch, much to our discomfort.

Three cheers for the alertness of this trained soldier, who had fought in the campaigns of North Africa and Greece!

The next day's march was tough going, the hardest so far, over rough mountainous country, gullies and ridges all the way, but for all that, the area had a certain appealing beauty to it. I thought if only I were doing this in peacetime, I would maybe appreciate it more, instead of being beset by the anxiety that hung over us in our mad scramble through this beautiful land.

A wonderful sight, about midday, as flight after flight of our heavy bombers passed overhead on their way to targets in Germany. As they were coming from the south, we thought they must have flown from Italy, and looking up at them, I could not but help thinking that in three or four hours' time, most of them (that is, the lucky ones) would be back at their own mess.

But then who were the lucky ones, the bomber crews or us? On reflection, I thought that the stakes might be more even than they appeared. Yes, if we were recaptured we would in all probability be shot, but some of those fliers might be shot down on their next mission and killed.

'Come on Bill, let's get going. There's a lot of ground to cover,' I said.

'Let's see if we can beat those boys home,' said Bill with a grin, pointing upwards.

We stood on a ridge, looking out across the open country ahead to the far-distant, pine-clad hills, and decided to rest up for the day. The countryside was dotted with villages, and it would be too risky to venture out in the open, so there and then we selected a hidden shelter in the forest and settled down to await nightfall.

We started our march about midnight, and it was tough-going all the way. Finally, just on dawn, we reached the top of what appeared to be a very high plateau, and on breasting the last steep rise, came upon what to me was the most poignant scene so far in all our wanderings, one I will never forget.

Before us was a large clearing in the forest. The early morning mists were starting to clear, the sun just beginning to stream between the tree trunks. Grazing peacefully were a dozen or more sheep, but what caught my eye was a young girl of about 12 or 13, standing motionless and leaning on a big shepherd's crook. She was dressed in a long skirt and a man's coat that reached half-way down her legs. An old hat was pulled well down on her head and long curls reached to her shoulders.

The peaceful scene before us stopped us in our tracks. The emotion I felt on seeing this serene picture is summed up by this little poem:

> Oh little girl, standing still and forlorn,
> How I wish the whole world could see
> You standing alone, in the pale mists of dawn,
> A silent symbol of man's history.
> Has your dad gone away to fight the fight
> For freedom and what he thinks best?
> No searching of soul to proclaim his right,
> When just issues are put to the test.
> And as we view this tranquil scene,
> The horrors of war slip away,
> And this quiet little girl is lost in a dream,
> Perhaps of a happier day.

On our approach, she shrank back with a startled look on her face and big, round, beseeching eyes, but made no attempt to run away. As Bill and I walked slowly towards her, we smiled and said, 'dobré jitro, slečno' (good morning, girlie), to which came a very quiet reply, 'dobré jitro, pane' (good morning sir). We lowered our packs to the ground, and Bill rummaged in his whilst I tried as best I could to allay any fears that might remain with this little girl. Meanwhile, Bill cut his oatmeal cake in half, and holding it out at arm's length, waited patiently.

A little hand came slowly out of the long sleeve and gently took his peace offering. 'Dekuji vam pane' (thank you sir), she said, and putting the cake in her mouth, she nibbled away, the while looking at us with those beautiful brown eyes. The expression on her face after the first mouthful was a picture, and we knew she had not tasted chocolate in a very long time, if at all. 'Velmi dobré' (very good), she said, then after another mouthful, she took a small white handkerchief from her pocket and carefully wrapped it round the remainder of the cake, then pointing to it she said, 'matka' (mother) and slipped it back into her pocket.

After resting awhile and having a snack ourselves, we shouldered our packs, and saying goodbye, we gave her a gentle kiss on the cheek and made towards the timberline. Then like the mists around us, we drifted away, stopping briefly to turn and wave to the pathetic little figure, who raised one arm in reply, the other still holding the shepherd's crook, making a serene picture in this idyllic setting.

We knew by now that the Hungarian border could not be far away, and as we stood at the edge of the forest, we could see a small village and beyond it what appeared to be either a river or a large canal. On the far bank were two soldiers with what appeared to be automatic rifles slung over their shoulders. Behind them a large plain stretched away to the far horizon.

We waited in the trees till dark, then camped in a haystack we'd spotted that afternoon by the water, pulling the straw over us before going to sleep. Next morning, we peered out cautiously to see if the two soldiers were still patrolling the far bank, but there was no sign of them, so we crawled out, stretched ourselves, and walked around to limber up, feeling much refreshed after the good night's sleep. If only we had known what was to follow in the next hour or so, I think we would have stayed in the haystack for the rest of the day before continuing our march.

I felt my chin, and looking at Bill, whose face also had a fair amount of growth, I said, 'Let's have a shave. We look like a couple of brigands.'

Squatting by the water's edge, we had started to shave when we suddenly heard voices, and before we had time to pack, we were surrounded by a crowd of people — men, women and young kids from the nearby village. Shrugging our shoulders, however, we decided to go on shaving, much to the amusement and giggles of the onlookers.

This was a situation we had not anticipated, and as we packed our gear, we discussed what to do next. Our minds were made up for us, however, when a fairly well-dressed man, who had an air of authority about him and seemed to be quite important, sorted himself out from the crowd, which quickly made way for him. He halted in front of us and spoke in clipped, hurried tones, but seeing by the expression on our faces that we did not understand him, he gestured with his right arm, bidding us follow him, and Bill and I thought it wise to comply with his wishes.

So here we were marching down the main street of the village, surrounded by the whole population, when suddenly a short, dark, nuggety-looking man fell into step alongside me and began to pull on my sleeve, whispering, 'Gehen Sie nicht, Gestapo' (Do not go, Gestapo). He kept repeating this phrase and I could see by the urgency of his manner and the look of concern and anxiety on his face, that he was in deadly earnest.

By now, Bill had heard what he was saying, especially his frantic warnings about the Gestapo, so when the stranger said, 'Kommen Sie mit!' (Come with me), we decided to depart, and the three of us dashed down a narrow lane to the accompaniment of loud shouts of 'Halt, halt' from our very important gentleman. But there was no stopping Bill and me, and we sped away like greyhounds after our friend, whilst the villagers blocked the laneway to prevent pursuit.

We raced through a field of corn, then trudged several miles through a pine forest to another village, where we were hidden in a cellar under an old house and told to remain absolutely quiet. Some hours later (we guessed around nightfall) we heard footsteps descending into the cellar, and when a lantern was lit, we could see several men. After introducing ourselves, we all sat around the walls and the leader of the group, who spoke fairly good English, handed each of us a parcel. The others had already opened their parcels, which turned out to contain the usual sustaining bread and cheese, and they handed round several bottles of plum brandy, the leader saying to Bill and me with a grin, 'We have no table to put you under when the bottles are finished.'

And with that, Ján, as he was called, undid another large parcel. With a look of triumph and a flourish, he produced a short-wave radio, and sitting it on a box in the middle of the cellar, he twiddled the dials. Before long we heard a clear, precise, English voice saying, 'This is London calling in the overseas service of the BBC News.' Then followed a detailed account of the big battles being waged on the Western and Eastern Fronts, and battles against the Japanese in the Pacific. While the news was being read, the only sound to be heard in the small underground cellar was the pouring of plum brandy and the munching of bread and cheese. Looking round at these hard-working farmers, who were listening with intense interest, I thought once again what staunch and wonderful people they were to risk their lives for us.

When the news had finished, a babble of voices broke out. Ján held up his hand for silence, then proceeded to translate the news, to the satisfied grins all round, because the Germans were falling back, though stubbornly, on all fronts.

Our partisan friends kept us informed of the movements of the search parties which the Gestapo had organised after Bill and I made our hasty retreat from the village several miles away. After three days, they told us the search had been called off and it would be all right for us to continue our journey, but that we must take all precautions not to be seen. They also told us that the Hungarian border, which was about 15 miles away, was patrolled regularly by enemy soldiers, and they urged us not to cross Hungary, but to go east towards Russia and the Tatra Mountains, which are in north central Slovakia.

It was just on dark when Bill and I said goodbye, shaking hands all round, and telling the leader how grateful we were to them for hiding us and giving us food and shelter. His reply — 'We fight for the same cause, do we not?' — was typical of these brave people, who were determined to free their country of the occupying forces. We left them standing at the edge of the village, hands upraised in the V for victory sign, their wishes of good luck and safe journey ringing in our ears.

Once again we had bright moonlight to help us on our way. We strode away to the east, but once out of sight of the village, we halted in the pines and discussed our options.

'What do you think, Bill?' I asked. 'They seemed pretty adamant about not trying to cross Hungary.'

'I don't know, Basil,' said Bill. 'I'm for sticking to our original plan. I think that with hard marching, we could cross Hungary in no more than a fortnight.'

I made a mental note about 'hard marching,' and also thought we would need a bit of good luck on our side, crossing hostile and unfriendly territory.

'Okay, Bill,' I said. 'Let's give it a go.'

So we swung away to the south, marching through fields of corn, tobacco, clover and grapes, and we could not help but notice how much larger these farms were than the ones we had crossed so far on this journey, and also how rich and fertile was the soil.

On this part of the trip we encountered a strange, fascinating little animal that was no bigger than a guinea pig. Like the American prairie dog, they lived in small burrows in the ground, and believe you me, they had vicious little teeth and claws.*As we walked through their nesting grounds, the animals would emerge from their burrows and take flying leaps at us, and when I say flying, it was just that. On either side of their bodies, between the front and back legs, was stretched a wide membrane,

---

* These may have been birch mice, a genus of six species of rodents native to eastern and northern Europe and parts of Asia. Birch mice travel by leaping and some live in shallow burrows.

very similar to that of the flying squirrel. Bill and I became very adept at catching them in mid-flight, applying the toe of our boots to their bellies, at which they would give a little squeal and race back into their burrows.

That night found us across the flatlands and up into the pine-clad hills, where we decided to camp for the night. We woke next morning to bright sunlight and the sound of voices. On opening our eyes, we looked up into the faces of about a dozen men, all heavily armed, with rifles over their shoulders and revolvers tucked in their belts. One of the men had cocked his revolver and was pointing it straight at our heads.

I exchanged glances with Bill and said, 'Let's hope they're friends!'

'Can't you see?' said Bill with a wry grin. 'He's trying to shake hands.'

'You don't sound like Germans. What nationality are you?' asked the man holding the pistol. He spoke fairly good English, and didn't look too dangerous a character.

We explained who we were.

'And where are you going?' asked their spokesman, who by now had lowered his revolver, but still kept it cocked.

'We're going home for Xmas,' I replied, trying to look calm.

At that he threw back his head and roared with laughter, much to his companions' amusement, and when he had explained to them what I had said, they also burst into fits of laughter and gathered round Bill and me, slapping us on the back, saying, 'dobry', dobry'.

When we had shaken hands and the talking had died down, we seated ourselves in a circle and proceeded to munch on bread and cheese. Their spokesman, who seemed to be their leader, asked us in all seriousness where we were really headed, and on hearing that we intended to cross Hungary and join Tito's partisans, he shook his head and told us that the Hungarians were ill-treating the Allied airmen who had been shot down over their territory. He too advised us instead to go east, up towards the Tatra Mountains, but would not tell us why, just saying his friends were up there and it would be a lot safer than trying to cross Hungary.

During the course of the meal, the men handed Bill and me a large aluminium container and a spoon each. The contents of the container had a taste and flavour very similar to our natural yoghurt, and were quite refreshing, so after taking a few spoonfuls each, we handed it round the circle.

The meal finished, the leader stood up and told us that they had to be on their way, so shaking hands again, we bade each other goodbye and good luck. Before leaving, however, the leader spoke to two of his men, who then pulled their revolvers from their belts, added a spare clip of ammunition, and held them out to Bill and me, and although we protested and said they would need them more themselves, the leader said, 'Please take them. You may well have use for them in the days and weeks that lie ahead.' Reluctantly, we took the guns and put them in our haversacks, the whilst thanking the men for their gifts, but the leader held up his hands, saying, 'It gives us great pleasure to help you.' Then raising their arms in farewell, this bunch of partisans walked away through the pines.

'Good luck to you all,' Bill and I called after them.

*   *   *

We decided to walk in the daytime, and on the second day, while making our way through the forest, we came to a very thick patch of pines. Looking up, we noticed a large sign tacked on a tree. What flashed a warning to us, in big letters, was the word *Verboten* (forbidden), followed by what seemed to be a warning that this was strictly a military area and that any civilian found past this boundary was liable to be shot. Looking into the gloom of the dense pine forest, which had an eerie and sinister look about it, I had a feeling of apprehension.

'What do you make of this bloody sign?' I said to Bill.

Looking to left and right, we could see the forest stretching away into the distance, with signs tacked to the trees every few hundred yards. We lowered our packs to the ground, and seating ourselves, discussed the situation. In the end, Bill said, 'Let's give it a go and take a chance. It's too damned far to go round — we'll just have to keep our eyes open.'

'OK,' I said. 'That's just what I was thinking.'

So we rose to our feet, adjusted our packs, and plunged into the forest. We had only been going for about half an hour when we came to an even more thickly planted area of pines. Looking down a slope through the tree trunks, we could see a wide clearing in the forest. In the open space stood a long line of huts, but there was no one in sight, so we walked slowly and cautiously towards the end hut, passing between it and the forest, then followed a track until we came to a small-gauge railway line. As we were crossing the line, we looked away to the right and to our amazement we could see, by the side of the track and set into the side of the hill, huge iron doors spaced about twelve metres apart. The railway line curved away to the left and disappeared behind the lower growing trees.

I don't know about Bill, but I had a tingling in my spine and a deep feeling of foreboding and impending danger at finding ourselves in this dangerous situation.

'Struth, Bill,' I said anxiously, 'what do you make of this?'

Basil Brudenell-Woods
in 1940, his 'two booful
fron' teef' still intact.

Blue Thompson on parade, Palestine 1941. *(see page 21)*

The diary Basil kept as a POW and while on the run. The entry for the 28th reads '11 o'clock. Through the hole in the wall'.

Banská Bystrica in the 1940s.

Bill Irvine (left) with
the author in American
GI uniforms. Bari,
Italy. September 1944.

Basil back home in Sydney with his niece, June (Priestley) Hall. 1946.

'I don't know Basil, but it's obvious that it's bloody well *verboten*, and if we want to save our heads, we'd better get out of here in a damned hurry.'

Suddenly the sound of voices came to our ears from the track behind us, so quickly and quietly we hid in the bushes and waited, and presently two German soldiers with rifles over their shoulders went past. It was only then, on looking up, that we noticed that the whole area was surrounded by high watch-towers armed with machine-guns and manned by German soldiers.

'Let's get to bloody hell out of here, or we're goners,' I said.

Dressed in civilian clothes, carrying revolvers and Czech money, we would have had a hard job convincing them of our nationality, especially since we were in such a heavily guarded and secretive place. The saying, 'dead men tell no tales,' may well have applied to us!

Hurriedly retracing our steps, all the while expecting to be cut down by a burst of machine-gun fire, we managed to extricate ourselves, re-crossing the railway line and going out the same way by the side of the buildings. On reaching the edge of the forest, we looked back, and to our amazement, out from the huts came a dozen or more German soldiers, who lined up in two ranks, obviously about to go on duty.

As they say in the American movies, 'we sure burnt up the trail,' wasting no time in getting away from that place. We did not stop until we had put a few miles behind us, then taking off our packs, we flopped down amongst the thick pines, absolutely exhausted, and lay back wondering what devilish works were going on in that underground hideaway. While lying there, we heard the sound of planes, and peering up through the branches, we saw wave after wave of heavy bombers, which we assumed must be either British or American, since they were flying in a northerly direction towards Germany.

We were now in Slovakia, heading south, and after two days of very tough going over high and thickly wooded hills, we came down to the edge of the forest, where we halted, looking out on a wide, open plain stretching away into the distance.

What followed was like a movie scenario. Across the plain came a beautiful black horse at full gallop, a man sitting astride it as though born to the saddle. He reined the horse to a walk, and bending low over its back, he disappeared through a big archway at the rear of a long ranch-style dwelling only a few hundred yards from where we stood. Bill and I looked at each other, and we could tell what each was thinking: Should we take the risk?

'What do you think, Bill?' I said.

He looked at me with a grin and said, 'Well, Basil, we can only get killed for trying!'

We discussed the situation, and what finally made up our minds was the fact that we were down to our last few spuds and sugar beet, having finished the bread and cheese so kindly given us by our partisan friends. So we strolled over and went through the archway, and once again before us was a scene that could have come from an American western. In one corner was a beautiful horse tethered to a hitching rail; at the other end of the large, paved courtyard was a big wooden table at which were seated half a dozen women shelling beans. When we appeared, their chatter instantly ceased, and they eyed us with apprehension and concern.

Bill and I lowered our packs to the ground and approached the table, greeting the women with the usual 'dobry den'. There was dead silence, so we tried first English, then German, but to no avail. Then one of the women rose and went through the door at the back of the house, reappearing a few minutes later with a beautiful blonde girl about 20 years of age, and the tall, dark, handsome man who had ridden up on horseback and appeared to be the girl's father.

'Do you speak English?' I asked.

The two shrugged their shoulders and spread their upturned hands, so we tried again with 'Sprechen Sie Deutsch?' (Do you speak German?) whereupon they both looked very concerned, and the girl replied, 'Sie sind Deutsch, ja?' (You are German, yes?)

'Nein,' Bill and I replied. 'Wir sind Australisch.'

At this, the girl looked puzzled, and with disbelief written on her face, she said 'Nein, nein, alle Australisch sind schwarz.' (No, no, all Australians are black.)

So Bill and I had a good laugh before doing our best to teach her some Australian history in faltering German.

Having convinced them that we belonged to the Allied cause and were indeed escaped POWs from Germany, they sent the women away and laid out on the big wooden table a wonderful feed of soup, roast pork with vegetables, bread, cheese and coffee. As we were about to sit down, another man rode up, and hitching his horse to the rail, came over, and once Bill and I were introduced, we all took our seats.

During the course of the meal, the usual question arose. Our host asked, 'Wohin gehen Sie?' (Where are you going?) and my reply, 'Wir gehen heim für Weihnachten,' brought the usual uproarious laughter from around the table. The girl's father, speaking slowly in German, said that we'd better hurry as we had thousands of miles to travel.

So the meal progressed. Looking round the table, I realised once again what wonderful, hospitable people they were to risk their lives by harbouring us. From what Bill and I could make out, they were terribly worried that the Russians would occupy their country before the British and Americans arrived. What a sad plight for this proud and democratic nation. On the one hand, their partisans were fighting to free the country from German domination, and on the other, they had a real fear of being taken over by Communist Russia. What an unenviable position to be in. I felt very deeply for them.

When we told our hosts that we were going through Hungary to join up with Tito's guerrillas in Yugoslavia, or our own forces in Italy, they held up their hands saying, 'Nein, nein, gehen Sie nicht, gehen Sie nicht'. They told us — by gesticulation and by speaking German very slowly, so that we could understand — that Hungary was fighting on Germany's side, and that some of the Allied pilots who had been shot down had been treated very badly.

It was then that they told us that the day before, two German soldiers had been shot by partisans, and as a consequence the Germans were dispatching an armoured division into Slovakia, which up till then had been a buffer state between the German forces and Russia, with Father Tiso as head of state.

Like all the other Czechs we'd met before, they urged us to go east, up into the Tatra Mountains, but beyond that they would reveal no more. After they had given us enough bread and cheese and slices of ham to last us for several days, Bill and I thanked them for all they had done for us. We shook hands, and much to our surprise, we received a lovely kiss from the beautiful blonde, who had tears in her eyes. Then we shouldered our packs and went east.

Apparently we were not the only ones going in that direction, for the next day we saw people on horseback, bicycles and carts, making their way through the forests in an easterly direction. That night we camped in a haystack, pulling just enough straw over us to cover ourselves, but allowing us to breathe some fresh air.

Just on dawn, I was awakened by a rumbling noise and nudged Bill awake. We peered out through the straw and immediately froze, as not more than 30 yards away, on the dirt road, was a column of German Panzer tanks. Standing up in the first tank was a German officer, whom we took to be the commander of this long line of armoured vehicles and motorised troops.

Now we knew that it would be a race to get to the Tatra Mountains, for the tanks were also headed east. After waiting for about an hour for the tanks to get well out of sight, we decided to strike north-east to get ahead of the German force. We would take the advice of the partisans, but at the same time keep within striking distance of the Hungarian border, and should things not pan out too well in the next week or so, we would head for Italy or Yugoslavia.

Towards midday, we came across a little farm hidden away in a small valley. Sitting at a small table in the garden was an elderly couple having a meal. Approaching, we spoke the usual greeting, 'dobrý den,' to which they replied in kind. We asked them if they spoke English and the old chap said, 'A little, I learn from friend of mine, schoolteacher,' and after introducing ourselves, they welcomed us with open arms, bidding us sit down and partake of the meal, which consisted of bread, cheese and yoghurt. To our surprise, there was also a leg of pork, from which he carved us a good helping, saying, 'Not for damned Germans,' and although we all had a good laugh at this remark, Bill and I knew that this grand old couple was living under the threat of the newly arrived German forces, who had not yet found this idyllic spot.

During the meal, the old chap said to us, sweeping his arm towards the horizon, 'Australia very far away, where do you go from here?' My usual reply made him chuckle; he apparently thought it a great joke. Although Bill and I were always amused at the response to these words, I think by now we had almost convinced ourselves that maybe, one day, we *would* be home for Xmas.

To my surprise, the old chap pointed to me and said, 'You have face to go round world!'

Taken aback at this unexpected remark, I said, 'I don't know about that, but we *are* half way round, and when we get back home, it will make the round trip.'

He roared with laughter, and turning to his wife, translated what the conversation was all about, and once more they burst into laughter. When the meal was finished and we had talked awhile, Bill and I said we would be on our way, so without another word, the old chap bent over the table and cut several slices of pork, and taking what remained of the bread and cheese, he wrapped them all in brown paper and handed them to us with a word of warning: 'Be careful, German patrols not far away.' We tried to refuse his offer, but he would not take no for an answer, so we thanked them and shaking hands, left them standing in their little garden, the old fellow with his arm around the shoulders of his wife, a lonely couple in a disturbed land, waving us a cheery goodbye, knowing we would never see them again.

We pushed on slowly for the lower Tatras, heading a little north by east but at the same time keeping the Hungarian border in mind. Again we found shelter for the night in one of those warm, all-concealing haystacks.

Things really warmed up the next morning. Shortly after moving off, we skirted a village and had not gone more than two or three hundred yards when we were stopped by a gorge, hundreds of feet in depth, with a swift-flowing river at the bottom. (We later found out that this was the Vah, a tributary of the Danube.)

We looked down into this unexpected, unwelcome obstacle, and I thought what damn back luck for this to happen just now, when we were in such a hurry to get ahead of the Germans.

Bill let out an oath, 'Now we're buggered!'

'No we aren't Bill,' I said, pointing to our right. 'Look over there.'

Not far away we saw what seemed to be a flying fox. Hurrying over, we climbed up on to a large platform, and there before us was a big wire cage about six feet by three and two feet deep, with wooden planks for flooring and iron plates at either end. The cage itself was suspended on two parallel wires stretched across the gorge. Inside the cage was a drum with a handle at one end; to the centre of the drum was attached a rope that ran across the gorge and was fixed to a platform on the other side.

'Come on,' said Bill, with urgency in his voice. 'Let's get a bloody move on before we get caught on this side of the river.'

So we quickly dumped our packs on the floor of our cage and jumped in. Bill grabbed the handle on the drum and began winding furiously, and the cage began to move slowly towards the other side of the gorge. Suddenly, from the direction of the village, came the sound of shouting, and looking over in that direction, I saw two German soldiers running out from behind the houses.

'We've got company,' I yelled to Bill.

'I can bloody well see that,' said Bill, winding away furiously on the handle. Meanwhile, the soldiers had taken their rifles from their shoulders, and kneeling down, began firing in our direction. There was the sound of bullets hitting the iron plate at the end of the cage.

'Get those revolvers out and give those bastards some of their own medicine,' yelled Bill. I quickly pulled the guns from the packs and returned their fire, hoping to prevent them from reaching the platform and stopping the flying fox. Suddenly, one of the soldiers let out a yell and started limping back towards the village, followed by his mate, who turned round a couple of times to let off a few rounds in our direction that fortunately fell short or wide of their mark.

'Good shooting, that will teach the bastards a lesson,' said Bill.

'More like a bloody fluke, but I reckon I could give John Wayne a run for his money.

'No damn time for romancing here, Basil,' said Bill. 'Let's get the hell out of this place.'

Just as he said this, the flying fox reached the far bank and we jumped out, quickly adjusted our packs onto our shoulders, and raced into the thickly wooded hills, not stopping for at least two hours. Finally, absolutely exhausted, we dropped down on the pine needles and lay there, hoping that we had eluded any German patrols that might have been sent after us. Enough is enough; we decided to call it a day, and finding a thick clump of pines, crawled into the middle of them and stayed there for the rest of the day and night.

Rising somewhat stiff the following morning, we had a snack of bread and cheese and some of the pork that our friends had given us. Once on our way, we swung into our usual stride, which we could carry on hour after hour. We were very fit.

*   *   *

WEDNESDAY, 30TH AUGUST. Sixty three days on the run. Somebody up there must like us. We wonder how much longer our good fortune will hold.

The day was a good one as we travelled over maize, clover and lucerne country. The farms were much larger than those we had passed through in Moravia, and there were larger herds of cattle, mainly dairy. The people we met in the fields (who were ever so friendly and helpful) told us that they were not rationed in any way, living mainly off their farms, which seemed to be thriving under their good management.

Towards sundown, we came across a farmer and his wife hoeing between rows of corn. The couple told us we were 20 miles from the Hungarian border and pointed out the small town of Tyrnau,* which they indicated we must avoid, as there were German troops in the vicinity. We made a detour around the town and at dusk came across a haystack,

---

* The names of the small towns and villages in this part of the narrative are written as they appear in my diary. We learned these names from people we met along the way, but some of the names were not on our map, so I wrote them as they were pronounced. I found out later from a Czech friend of mine that the Germans had changed a lot of the names from Czech to German when they took over the country.

where we decided to camp for the night.

The next three days were very similar. The going was good over these wonderfully fertile and rich farmlands, and although we were down to living on vegetables and fruit, we were in terrific nick, enjoying these days of hard slogging, with the smell of growing crops all around us. Scarecrows dotted the landscape, and since Bill had lost his cap, we were very interested in them, but none were wearing headgear of any shape or form and Bill muttered to himself, 'They must be bloody scarce round these parts.' Once again we came across those strange little animals with the sharp teeth and claws, and as before we sent them scurrying with the toe of our boots.

All this time we were travelling almost parallel to the Hungarian border, which was a few miles to the south. Many field workers along the way helped by giving us bread and cheese and warning us of any German patrols in the area.

We passed the towns of Voderady and Mal Hostice, sleeping in haystacks each night, and at a place called Uhrovec, we met a band of partisans, a great bunch of young men who shared their rations with us, saying they could get any amount of food from their friends all round the country. With them was a Slovakian chemical expert and his wife, who both spoke fairly good English. They told us they had left the town of Trencin with what they stood up in, just five minutes before the Germans took over the place, and were now staying with relatives.

After thanking our friends, we said our good-byes, and for the next three days marched across farms and forest lands, noting the large size of the holdings and the numerous horse-drawn carts. Once we sighted a beautiful, sparkling landau pulled by two magnificent black horses. Sitting up front was the coachman or driver, and reclining gracefully on the back seat was a beautiful, elegantly dressed woman. As they disappeared across the plain, leaving a cloud of dust behind them, I could not help but wonder at the great contrast to the events occurring all over this German-occupied country.

About mid-morning on the third day after leaving the partisans, we came across a small settlement hidden away in a little valley and surrounded by well-kept vegetable gardens, rows of sugar beet, and cows grazing in fields of clover. Taking a chance, we approached some workers who were chipping weeds in the sugar beet, and with a cheery grin we bade them 'dobrý den' and tried to explain who we were.

Work ceased and all eyes turned in our direction. We could clearly see a look of concern on the faces of some of these workers, and one of them, who seemed to be in charge, walked over to us and returned our greeting, then shouldering his hoe, beckoned us to follow him. As we approached the village, we could not help noticing how well-kept the cottages were, everything spick and span.

A small group of people, who had obviously seen us coming from afar, came out from the end of the village to meet us. Their spokesman, a wonderful fellow whom we found out later to be in charge of the settlement, introduced himself as Tibor Stern. He spoke very good English, and when he found out who we were, he welcomed us with open arms and conducted us down a road lined with cottages. We were ushered into a large building, a mess hall for the whole village, and Tibor bade us be seated at one of the long tables.

All this time we were surrounded by a crowd of very excited and talkative people. We heard Tibor Stern giving orders in the kitchen as he rustled up a meal for us. The chattering and noise died down as he came out of the kitchen followed by a number of his helpers, all carrying food of some description.

'There you are, you fellows,' said Tibor. 'You must be damned hungry, get your teeth into that and we will talk later.' What a meal! Beautifully cooked vegetables, soup, bread, cheese and hot coffee, all of which we enjoyed with much relish.

Tibor told us that this was Kostelany, a Jewish settlement, and that they had been here for three years. Bill and I gathered it was a concentration camp which until a few days ago was under strict supervision by the ruling authority, who had left the camp suddenly, without warning.

Tibor was very worried. They had heard about the German armoured column coming in their direction, and were now waiting for some trucks to take them to a place called Banská Bystrica, up in the lower Tatra Mountains.

(We learned later that a Slovak republic had been proclaimed at Banská Bystrica, in central Slovakia, on September 1. This major uprising involved both army and partisans, and covered much of the country. It explained why the Jewish camp had been abandoned by its guards; the tanks we'd met along the way must have been a vanguard of the German counterattack.) [See the Appendix for details of this uprising.]

It was years since I had seen such a happy crowd of people, even though they had the threat of the gas chambers in Poland hanging over their heads. This said a lot for Tibor, who had a wonderful personality. From what Bill and I could see, he also had a terrific organising ability, was highly intelligent, cheerful at all times, and was an absolutely ideal leader to be in charge of this Jewish settlement.

After the meal, Tibor showed us to a room with a couple of bunks, and it was then that the richness of the meal started to bring on a touch of the trots. I spent most of the afternoon on the loo, whilst Bill, who did not seem to be upset with my complaint, was shown round the camp by Tibor. If Bill and I had but known what was in store for us the following morning, maybe we would not have slept so soundly, but sleep we did that night — the best we'd had in months.

The next morning we were awakened by the sounds of shouting and much running backwards and forwards outside. All was confusion, and above Tibor's frantic shouting we could hear the noise of engines being revved. Bill and I sat straight up, listening intently.

'Struth, it's the bloody German tanks. Let's get out of here through the windows,' said Bill, throwing off his blanket.

'Those engines don't sound heavy enough for tanks,' I said. Just then, Tibor rushed into our room shouting, 'Grab your packs, the trucks have arrived. The Germans are only a few miles away. Please hurry.'

We needed no second bidding, and jumping from our bunks, we grabbed our packs and raced outside to the waiting trucks. What a sight! People running in all directions, carrying what goods and articles of clothing they could manage, throwing them onto the backs of the trucks then clambering up after them.

Tibor was there racing up and down, giving orders, with an urgency in his voice that bespoke the seriousness of the situation. He beckoned to us and pointed to a truck, yelling, 'Hurry, the Germans are coming fast.' So we threw our packs over the tailboard of the truck and hauled ourselves up onto the vehicle, ably assisted by many willing hands. Finally, Tibor gave the order to move off and the trucks roared away out of the camp. Bill and I, who were in the last truck, could see dust rising from German tanks just a few miles away and approaching fast.

We travelled all that day, passing Nováky and Handlova, gradually getting higher and higher into the hills. Handlova had a mainly German population, which seemed somewhat hostile, so we raced through that town and pushed on, arriving at our destination in the late afternoon.

8
Banská Bystrica

SEPTEMBER 9, 1944. Here we are at last in the small town of Banská Bystrica, nestled away in a valley surrounded by high hills. *This* must be the destination that our friends along the way had been urging us to make for.

On getting down from the trucks, we were immediately taken to partisan headquarters and kept in a room until summoned by two armed guards. We followed them down a long corridor and were ushered into a large room. Just outside the door, I noticed four very young German soldiers in camouflage uniforms, standing under guard. What struck me most about them was their very arrogant, truculent manner; I surmised they were most probably some of Hitler's *Jugend* (youth) contingents.

The first words we heard on entering the room were 'Welcome to Banská Bystrica, gentlemen,' spoken in perfect English. Rising from his chair on the far side of a large desk was a tall, dark, handsome man, well over six feet. He came round to our side of the desk, shook hands with Bill and me, and pointing to two chairs, said, 'Please be seated'. He went back, sat down facing us, and leaning back in his chair, he said, 'Well, Bill and Basil, our mutual friend Tibor Stern has related the story of your escape. Now would you please tell me a little about yourselves — your credentials, regiment, etc.'

Turning my head, I looked at Bill, and knew he was thinking the same thing: should we give him all this information? Then I thought, what the heck, he must be on the right side of the fence, and just as Bill nodded his head, a voice interrupted my thoughts.

'I know what you are thinking, but believe me, I'm in charge of the partisans for the whole of this region and for their protection I have to verify your identities.'

'How will you do that?' I asked.

'We have our ways and means,' he replied.

Looking at him, I could see the sincerity and honesty written on his face, so Bill and I gave him our names, ranks and numbers, and told him in which theatres of war we had become POWs, after which he rose from his chair, saying, 'Thank you for this information. Now you will be shown to your sleeping quarters. Please do not leave them until you have seen me tomorrow morning.' And shaking hands, he passed us over to the armed guard who was standing just inside the door (and who, I noticed, never took his hand away from the trigger of his gun).

We were taken to a large nearby house that had been converted into barracks during this recent uprising. We were ushered into a big lounge, and to our pleasant surprise, we were greeted by about a dozen American airmen who had been shot down in bombing raids over the country. What a grand lot of chaps they were, making us feel quite at home. After introducing themselves, they produced some real coffee and we sat around chatting into the early hours until finally, nearly dropping asleep where we sat, we were shown to our room. We took off our boots, flopped down on our bunks, and fell sound asleep.

The following morning we were again taken to headquarters, and on entering the room where we were questioned the day before, our new-found friend rose from his chair, saying, 'I have found out that all that you have told me is correct, that you really are Australians'.

'Yes, fair dinkum Aussies,' said Bill with a grin.

A puzzled look came over the partisan leader's face and he said, 'What is that word dinkum?'

We explained that it was a slang word meaning real, so with a smile he said, 'That's for sure, as I found out from London. And now I will give you a legitimation, or as you would call it, an identification pass, which you must carry at all times, and also 3000 koronas or crowns.' He went on to say, 'You are very lucky. Tomorrow we hope to have two planes coming in from southern Italy, bringing in supplies, guns and ammunition for the partisans. You and the American airmen will be flown back to your own lines.'

We could hardly believe our ears; the thought of being with our own troops was quite overwhelming. We shook hands with this tall imposing leader and thanked him for all the trouble he was taking on our behalf, and before we left, I asked him his name, to which he replied, 'I do not have a name, just a number. I think you will understand.' (We found out later that he was a Czechoslovakian who had been dropped by parachute the week before, after being flown out from Scotland.) So we left him standing by the desk with a smile on his face, his 'good luck' ringing in our ears as we went out the door.

*　　　*　　　*

The two planes did not arrive as expected the following day and we were left wondering if something untoward had happened to prevent their arrival. We were now free, however, to wander round the town, so with some of the airmen acting as our guides, we set out to explore.

One of the airmen, a university graduate and a fairly brainy chap to boot, gave us a rundown on Banská Bystrica, which he said he'd been doing a bit of research on by reading and by talking to some of the local leading lights. He told us that the town dated from the 13th Century, and was noted for its copper and silver mines. The area itself had been invaded in turn by Tartars and Turks, and was then under Hungarian rule for a thousand years, but despite all these invasions, the Slovaks had kept their identity and their language.

To the north of the town the Carpathian Mountains swept away up into Poland; to the east lay the Tatra Mountains. Banská Bystrica itself was situated on the Hron River, in the Lower Tatras, and had a population of around 12 000. From what I could make out, the town was laid out more or less in the shape of an oblong. Our historian pointed out a very tall square tower rising above the town, seemingly part of a big building which looked like a church, and he informed us that it was built by the Catholics hundreds of years ago. This tower, or bell-tower as he called it, not only summoned people to prayer but also served as a watch-tower to warn the village of an approaching enemy.

The houses themselves were very old, and there were quaint little shops lining the square. People sat drinking coffee at small tables in crowded cafes, chatting no doubt about the latest news of the German advance, and although life seemed to be going on normally enough, we could see the underlying anxiety in the faces of the elderly, who were probably wondering what would happen should the Germans occupy the town.

Half-way down one side of the square was Wagner's Restaurant, where we had a number of meals when not eating back at the barracks. There were also some small refreshment shops where we used to drool over ice cream and cakes. Just think of that! Dishing up those luxuries up to Bill and me, who had not seen or eaten anything like this in years and were as lean and muscular as greyhounds.

Wagner's Restaurant! What a meeting place — all types and characters, a multitude of nationalities. What stories of danger and heroism were unfolded to us, some of them very sad and poignant; those that follow are exactly as they were related to me and written down in my diary.

On that first day in Wagner's, we met a Polish partisan girl dressed in khaki, with a revolver strapped to her waist. She had been very well-educated before the war and spoke perfect English, but was now living in the mountains with four other girls and some hundred men, all of them partisans. Her mother had been killed and she didn't know what had become of the rest of her family, and as she told us her story, tears were running down her cheeks. What sadness.

Another day we met three Poles who had escaped into Hungary but had been interned until the Germans occupied their country. They were then transported towards the killing factories in Poland, where at such places as Lublin and Birkenau, as many as thirty thousand people were gassed in one day. These Poles were fortunate to escape by jumping off the train; they were probably the only ones left alive of the whole trainload. To what depths can men sink, that they would treat fellow humans in such ways?

A couple of days later, Bill and I were sitting in Wagner's when a beautiful girl walked into the café. We invited her to our table to have some coffee and cakes with us, and to our (and especially my) pleasure, she slid quietly onto the seat alongside me. To cap it all she spoke good English.

Alexeja Ottlekova was her name — one of the most charming and intelligent girls that I have ever had the pleasure to meet. Like the others, she told us her story — how she and her mother, a Doctor of Medicine, had walked over the mountains from Zilina, taking from their house only what they could carry (which in their case included, besides personal possessions, a carton of cigarettes and a 50-year-old map). Her mother had studied at the University of Prague and also at Bratislava; her father was living in the mountains with the partisans. She recounted all this in a matter-of-fact way, as though it was nothing unusual, and when we had finished our coffee, she invited us to have tea with her mother and herself at the hospital.

Like mother, like daughter! What a lovely, charming personality was this Doctor of Medicine who greeted us that night at the entrance to the hospital and ushered us into a small dining room, and what a meal she had prepared for us! First she poured some white wine into beautiful crystal glasses; a magnificent flavour — we hadn't sampled anything like it in years. Then followed a beautifully cooked dinner of roast fowl and trimmings and a delicious dessert of peach pie and cream.

You can just imagine how we felt, sitting down to such a wonderful home-cooked meal, the like of which we had not tasted in many a long day. All through the meal, we were plied with questions about our homeland: where we lived, the Aborigines, kangaroos, and especially about our cities. The wine flowed, our tongues loosened, and by the end of the meal, Bill and I felt that we had known them for years, and pressed them to come to Australia and visit us after the war. Then after thanking them for a wonderful meal, we kissed them goodbye, and in the early hours slowly made our way back to our quarters through the quiet streets of the small, beleaguered town of Banská Bystrica.

Each night at barracks and particularly on this night, after such great hospitality, Bill and I would do a lot of soul-searching: should we join the partisans or take the plane back to our own lines? The decision was not an easy one, for our feelings ran strongly in both directions.

On the one hand, we had been prisoners for years and had not seen our folks for a long time. In addition, our boys were still fighting the Japanese in the Pacific islands, and we were anxious to rejoin our regiments. On the other hand, here were these partisans, and Tito's guerillas in Yugoslavia, locked in a struggle with the same enemy as our own. Was there any difference between this part of the world and the other side of the globe, when it was all for the common cause?

That night, before turning in, Bill and I decided that if the plane did not arrive in the next few days, we would throw in our lot with the partisans. But lying there in my bunk in the darkness, and overriding all our discussions, was the picture of the beautiful face of Alexeja. I could not get her out of my mind; maybe I had been too long away from the company of women.

We were a noisy crowd in Wagner's the following day, and what an assembly! The American airmen looked pretty dashing in their Air Force uniforms and were (of course) accompanied by a bevy of beautiful girls who seemed to have fallen hook, line and sinker, not only for their uniforms, but also for their American accent. There were also Poles, Jews and other nationalities who had fled in advance of the German occupation.

As Alexeja, Bill and I sat there, it gave me a great feeling of well-being to be mixing with such friendly people, and particularly with our hosts the Czechs, who had been one of the great democratic nations of Europe until Hitler marched in and took away most of their freedoms, but not their spirit or their strong determination to survive, come what may. They were living for the day when the Allies would defeat Germany, and looking forward to welcoming the British and American troops. They were terribly worried about the Russians, however, and praying that our troops would arrive before those of the East.

We were joined at our table by a well-dressed elderly gentleman who appeared to be in his sixties. He told us he was a lawyer, and went on to say that he had been a prisoner for five years during the last war and in 1920 had acted as interpreter to the American mission at Vladivostok.

The loud conversation, the babble of voices and the friendly atmosphere in the restaurant reminded me so much of the outside bar in the famous beer garden of the old Newport Hotel at Pittwater, about 20 miles north of Sydney, where in the summer, of a Friday or Saturday afternoon and evening, the sound of voices was deafening and one might see film stars and famous characters from all over Australia and the other side of the world. Presiding over all, like a master of ceremonies, was the well-known Tim Bristow, who was there to put a restraining hand on the drunk and disorderly. One Saturday afternoon, Tim and his brother fought a very bloody fight with several opponents, and between them they flattened the lot. That fight was talked about for many a day.

Each afternoon, after adjourning from the cafe, we would join most of the townsfolk, young and old alike, in a general parade, walking down one side of the square and back up the other, the young men ogling the girls and vice versa. I knew this was the custom in some of the western countries of Europe such as Spain, Italy and France, but did not think it would extend so far east.

*   *   *

16 SEPTEMBER. This afternoon we were invited to a party at a Mrs. Chekov's house. Mrs. Chekov was born in Slovakia and had lived for some years in America, but was now living in Banská Bystrica. What a delightful person. She had gone to no end of trouble to make us all feel at home. Her big lounge was a picture of loveliness: deep wall-to-wall carpets, comfortable leather-covered lounge, with chairs to match, while on the walls hung beautiful paintings, originals done by well-known artists. Over in one corner was a table whose legs must have been groaning under the weight of those plates of delightful sandwiches and a wonderful variety of delicious cakes, plus of course the usual bottles of wine and plum brandy.

Mrs. Chekov and Alexeja acted as hostesses, and Bill and I handed round the plates. As usual our American friends were surrounded by a crowd of very pretty and admiring girls. Boy, what I'd have given for one of those smart-looking uniforms!

About half-way through the afternoon, when the party was going full-swing, a young Czech came into the room, and walking over to Mrs.

Chekov, spoke to her in a low voice, whereupon she held up her hand for silence. After introducing us all to the young chap, she told us that he had just heard that the partisans had caught two Gestapo men at the railway station. The Germans had been dressed as women and had intended to poison Banská Bystrica's water supply (nice people). I guess they will be given short shrift by the higher command.

This bit of news had a sobering effect on us all and made us realise to what extent those Gestapo villains would go to achieve their evil ends. The incident was the main topic of conversation as we stood around in small groups, discussing and wondering what would be the enemy's next move.

The party went on well into the night, the Americans holding centre stage as far as the bevy of beautiful girls were concerned (including Alexeja, who was part of the adoring audience, hanging on to every word that the handsome airmen had to say). I can still picture vividly that gay scene in the beautiful lounge in far-off Czechoslovakia. Although we did not know it at the time, the party was the last we were to have before being scattered to different parts of the globe.

On returning to barracks, whom should we see? None other than Scotty — what a pleasant surprise! Bill and I shook hands with him and introduced him to our American friends. But what of Gordon? Scotty told us that they had separated, but would not say what had happened between them. We did not press the subject any further, and to this day I still do not know the answer.

*   *   *

17 SEPTEMBER 1944. I will never forget that date. Dramatic, poignant and exhilarating.

About mid-morning, Alexeja, Bill, I, and a couple of the American boys were strolling down National Road when all of a sudden a truck from the flying school came racing up and pulled in alongside us. Hanging over the tailboard were an American airman and Scotty, who yelled out excitedly, 'Jump up, you blokes, we're going to the airfield, the planes are here.'

Turning to Alexeja, I said, 'This looks like goodbye. I'm going to miss you, but I'll write to you after the war,' and with a lump in my throat, I threw my arms around her and gave her a lingering kiss, which was returned with feeling. I could see tears welling up in her eyes.

'I'll miss you also, Basil. Please write to me.'

The boys in the truck were meanwhile yelling to us to hurry, so Bill and I and the other two men scrambled over the tailboard, assisted by

112

Scotty and one of the Americans, and flopped onto the floor. Gazing back, the last I saw of Alexeja was a lonely figure standing forlornly in the middle of the road waving a poignant farewell.

Bill and I thought we had left all our belongings behind, but not so. In the mad rush to board the trucks, one of the Americans had remembered our packs and picked them up, for which we were very grateful. On the way to the airfield, the boys told us that there were two B17 Flying Fortresses at the landing ground. I could hardly believe my ears. At long last it seemed that I was on my way home.

Sure enough, when we arrived, there were two lovely war birds standing on the airfield with their engines running, while overhead circled two or three long-range fighters that were acting as escorts and giving protective cover to the bombers on the ground.

Never had I seen such a wonderful sight. Clustered round both planes were a large number of men. They had almost finished unloading what looked like large cases of ammunition and foodstuffs, which they had stacked a little way from the aircraft in separate dumps and loaded onto waiting trucks.

And who should be standing there supervising the whole operation? None other than the tall, handsome partisan leader who had interrogated us at his headquarters on our arrival at Banská Bystrica. He finished giving his orders and walked over to where we were standing, then with a smile shook hands with us all, and said with a grin, 'Well, boys, this looks like our farewell. I wish you a safe journey, and may you all soon be back with your families, not forgetting you fair dinkum Aussies.'

Once again we thanked him for all he had done for us, and oh, how I wished that I could have known his name and address, but such was not to be. We were divided into two groups — Bill and myself and some of the American airmen in one plane, and Scotty and the rest in the other. Also boarding our plane were some men dressed in civilian clothes, a very secretive lot who kept to themselves and didn't speak to anyone; I guessed that they must be in the intelligence service.

'See you in Italy, Scotty,' I yelled.

'At lang last, we're ganging awa' he shouted from the steps of his plane, with a cheery grin and a wave.

We climbed the steps leading up into the plane, and on the top step I turned to look back at the wonderful Czech who was standing there looking up at us, waving and giving the V for victory sign. A feeling of sadness came over me and I had a great desire to race down the steps and join the partisans in their fight.

My thoughts were rudely interrupted as I was taken by the arm and pulled into the plane by one of the crew. The steps were withdrawn, the door slammed shut as the roar of the engines started to increase, and the plane moved slowly forward down the runway, rising smoothly like the flight of a big pelican taking off from a lonely river or lagoon.

Sad to relate, it was only about a week later that we heard that Banská Bystrica had fallen to the Germans. The partisans' brave leader was killed in the fighting, and although to me he was only a number, I'm sure his name will go down in the history of Czechoslovakia.

*   *   *

Postcript to Chapter 8

The flight from Banská Bystrica is described on pp. 188-189 of *SOE: An Outline History of the Special Operations Executive 1940-46,* by M. R. D. Foot (University Publications of America, Inc., 1986):

> ... one of the war's odder semi–clandestine operations, a landing by two B-17 Flying Fortresses at Tri Duby, a small grass airfield between Banská Bystrica and Zvolen in central Slovakia on 18 September. Forty-one P-51 Mustang fighters were in attendance as escort, and flew to and fro for the twenty-five minutes the big aircraft were on the ground.
>
> Half a dozen Russian staff officers, previously put in by the Soviet air force, were in attendance on the airfield, and showed keen interest in every detail of the B-17s ... The two aircraft ... brought in four and a half tons of military stores and an OSS mission, and flew out to Bari a delighted party of twelve Americans and three British airmen, and a Czech.

A footnote identifies a number of the Americans, and tells how they came to be in Banská Bystrica. The 'three British airmen' are obviously Basil, Bill and Scotty, for there was only one other of such flight into (and out of) the town during the uprising, on October 7. On that occasion, another 28 Americans and 'a couple of New Zealand privates' were able to hitch a ride to safety. Basil has no memory of the large number of escort planes mentioned above, and indeed it seems highly unlikely that 41 Mustang fighters would be spared for such a long flight. (Ed.)

9
Freedom

What a powerful word! I don't suppose that any word in the course of history has embodied so much meaning, inspired such strong purpose, or engendered such depth of feeling. Born from the wishes and desires of those in human bondage — the toiling slaves who raised the pyramids, the road gangs of the Roman Empire, the tens of thousands who struggled and died to build the magnificent Great Wall of China — freedom in time became the desire not only of individuals, but of whole nations of people who rose to defend their way of life, refusing to be subservient to the men wielding the whips.

But one man stood up and cast a deep shadow over the Earth, saying, 'My neighbours do not think after my fashion, I shall free them from their misguided thoughts,' and in so doing, he slaughtered millions in a terrible Holocaust, a blot on history for all time. But the nations refused to be freed in such a manner, and the man was put in his place, but not before he had created chaos and sorrow in many lands, spread distrust and suspicion throughout the nations of the world, and sowed the seeds of the Cold War.

So you can see that our freedom (and by 'our' I mean Bill and me, and those Americans sitting alongside us in the plane) pales into insignificance when compared with the despair of the millions who took that one-way train ride to the Holocaust in Poland. Our flight to freedom was a small, personal affair, a release from that inner circle of barbed wire. We were lucky enough to have the means to hop over that huge, grim, warring outer circle of nations and rejoin our comrades in the free world, whereas those condemned souls in the cattle trucks had no circles big or small to go through or over, only a train bearing them towards a dark tunnel from which there was no escape.

I have flown in planes since, been shouted at by that excellent instructor Vic Schuback, who was trying to teach me to fly Tiger Moths at the Royal Aero Club at Bankstown, Sydney, but never have I experienced anything like the thrill of getting into that big war bird. It was my first flight ever, under *such* sensational and exciting circumstances, and as those four powerful engines bore us steadily skywards, I thought, 'Well, this is it'. A great feeling of exhilaration swept over me, and looking at Bill and the American airmen, I knew by the look on their faces that their thoughts must have been very similar to my own. As we crossed the Hungarian border, my thoughts went back momentarily to the last three months — the factory and the mates we'd left behind, the hole in the wall, the frantic dash for freedom, and those wonderful friendly people who had sheltered the four of us in our hour of need.

Leaning back against the fuselage, I took stock of my surroundings and noted that the plane was all its name implied — a veritable Flying Fortress, with rapid-firing guns mounted on top, fore and aft, and below — and I felt a certain sense of security and protection against possible attacks by German fighters. Like the American eagle, this powerful bird had lethal talons.

One of the crew came back and asked Bill and me if we would like to come forward and have a look at Budapest, so we got to our feet and followed him forward to the cockpit, scrambling over piles of ammo boxes and our packs. What a great sight — the centuries-old city spread out below us, lying astride the beautiful, romantic River Danube, made famous in song and story.

The pilot pointed, and away to the right we could see Allied planes bombing fuel dumps on the outskirts of the city. Thick smoke from the burning oil spiralled thousands of feet into the air, showing us that our planes must have been right on target.

All this time we had been gaining height steadily, and by the time we reached the high mountains of Yugoslavia, we were up about 14 000 feet. Boy was it cold in our thin clothes, but as we shivered, I thought that this was a bloody sight easier than slogging across Hungary to join Tito's partisans, who were battling the Germans on the ground thousands of feet below us. From what the pilot told Bill and me, Tito and his courageous men were putting up an heroic fight against tremendous odds.

After crossing the mountains, we gradually descended to about 5 000 feet. and crossed the Adriatic, finally landing at Bari, in southern Italy, at about two thirty in the afternoon.

What a momentous day! Bill and I stepped down on to the runway, then stood there facing one another, and as our hands gripped, the look in our eyes said it all. To Bill's 'At long last, we've made it, Basil, old mate,' I replied, 'Well, Bill, after all our efforts, it looks as though we might be home for Xmas.' We both grinned, and the feelings we had could only be experienced by someone who had spent long years of boredom and frustration surrounded by barbed wire, wire that hemmed in one's everyday movements and thoughts.

We were met on the tarmac by none other than General Twining, who shook hands with us all and said to Bill and me, 'Great effort, boys. Congratulations on your escape, and welcome home.' What wonderful words, and what a nice guy.

Before leaving, Bill and I shook hands with the American friends we'd met at Banská Bystrica, and thanked the Captain and crew for the great job they'd done in saving us a hell of a lot of walking.

'Say, you guys,' said the Captain, 'we're just glad to give you some good service'.

What a great bunch those Yanks were. We said our good-byes to our American friends, hoping to see them again, but of course we never did, as they were in all probability flown back to the States for a well-deserved rest.

We did not hang around for long, but before leaving the airport, Bill and I looked to see if we could spot Scotty, but his plane was on another runway several hundred yards away. We reckoned we would catch up with him wherever we were going, but alas, we did not see him again; he must have been taken straight to British Headquarters and his own lines. We hoped that he was given leave back home.

We were taken by truck to a large American tent hospital on the outskirts of Bari, deloused, given hot showers and pyjamas, then paraded before the doctor, who declared us to be reasonably fit, although rather thin. He said he would keep us under observation for 24 hours, then directed the medical orderly to take us to one of the big convalescent tents.

Boy, what bliss, what meals, and that night Bill and I saw our first film in three and a half years. President Roosevelt appeared on the screen, talking about the war aims, but one could see that the war had taken a toll on his health. He looked terribly thin and drawn, and to judge from the comments of the American GI's sitting on either side of Bill and me, there was a general opinion that he wouldn't last very long. Sad to relate, their predictions proved to be only too correct, as he died the following year, the victory year in Europe, and many nations mourned him throughout the world.

We slept like logs between white sheets for the first time in many years, and the following morning, after a slap-up breakfast, we were issued with American GI uniforms and rubber-soled boots.

'You look like a god-damn Yank,' Bill said to me.

'Well,' I said, 'take a look at yourself. We're a couple of smart American Aussies, let's go out and get our photos taken.' So we got our leave passes and strolled round the town, and it was not long before we found a photographer. The accompanying photo speaks for itself (see photo section).

That afternoon we were picked up and taken to British intelligence headquarters for questioning, and it was with some regret that we left our new-found American friends. The officer in charge congratulated Bill and me on our escape, then opened a drawer and pulled out a large map, which he spread on top of his desk. He then proceeded to question us on our escape route and anything of importance that we had seen or heard during our march; he was particularly interested in those iron doors in the side of the hill where Bill and I were nearly caught, and in the train carrying guns and armoured vehicles towards the Eastern Front. Of course Bill and I were just as intrigued as the intelligence officer about what lay behind those iron doors, but we never found the answer.

During this interrogation, a high-ranking Royal Air Force (RAF) officer strolled into the room and asked the intelligence officer who we were. I could see the look of disappointment on his face as he said, 'Oh, I thought they might be some of my boys'.

I chirped in and said, 'Is there anything wrong with a couple of good Aussies?'

'No, no, not at all,' he said. 'Good on you chappies, great effort, congratulations,' and with that he turned and left the room.

'Struth, Basil,' said Bill, 'you stuck your neck out a bit'. Turning round, I saw our interrogating officer had a big grin on his face. 'Well,' he said, 'you are not lacking in something to say.'

I can understand why that Air Force officer would have thought that we were a couple of his airmen. You see, in most of the Allied POW camps of any size where RAF personnel were imprisoned, the Air Force boys ran a very well-organised committee that arranged nearly every escape attempt. Our escape, however, was a go-it-alone effort.

The interrogation over, the officer had some tea brought in, and we shared some rich currant cake which his family had sent out from England. It was delicious — hadn't tasted anything like it for years.

We chatted awhile and he asked us about our country, and we invited him to stay with us if he ever decided to visit Australia. A nicer chap you couldn't wish to meet. After a short time, he stood up and said he'd better get on with his work, and on shaking hands, I thought I had never said so many hellos and good-byes as in the past week — the people who come into your life, and just as quickly pass by and fade into memories.

When we got outside, a truck was waiting, so we hopped in and went back to the American tent hospital, collected our packs, and were then driven to Transit Camp 177. What a doss house — a big, rambling, old building with a hard concrete floor. We were given two blankets apiece and allocated a place to sleep, and looking at Bill, I knew we were both of the same mind. Dumping our packs, we turned and walked out.

'Christ,' said Bill, 'I'd rather be sleeping out under the pines'.

I wholeheartedly agreed, but at the same time I thought of those soldiers on active service, being toughened up before the poor buggers were thrown into the bloody battles raging to the north of us. What had we got to complain about, when they were destined for such a maelstrom? Bari at this time was one big staging camp for the Allied forces, who were gallantly battling their way up the peninsula. It included a huge aerodrome from which our airmen operated far and wide behind the enemy lines.

After leaving the camp, Bill and I found the New Zealand Club. Did those Kiwis welcome us with open arms! What terrific blokes! They wouldn't let us pay for anything, shouted us drinks and gave us New Zealand currency, with the jocular remark, 'What the hell do we want with that stuff? Where we're going, Aussie, we'll most probably use it for bum fodder.'

And of course there were those lovely girls who had joined the army back home in New Zealand and suddenly found themselves on the other side of the world. They were doing a great job in making that club a most enjoyable and happy rendezvous for the boys on leave and for those going on up to the front line. The Kiwis were quite concerned about our sleeping quarters and the fact that we were sleeping on concrete, and right or wrong, they insisted that Bill and I camp the night in their lines. They guaranteed us at least a straw palliasse or stretcher.

The temptation was very strong, but after the club closed for the night, Bill and I thanked our Kiwi hosts and returned to the transit camp. Lying down on that hard couch, my thoughts went back to similar conditions — the concrete floor in Tripoli.

Now, who should arrive very early the following morning? None other than our friend the intelligence officer of the previous day. He was most profuse in his apologies for our sleeping quarters, saying that there had been a mistake — we should have been taken to a rest camp about five miles outside Bari, near the aerodrome.

We were damned glad to hear this bit of news, and once again, after thanking the officer for his trouble, we clambered on to a truck and were driven to the rest camp, where we were put in Montgomery Wing (C), Hut 49. What a difference — beaut stretchers with mosquito nets, and on strolling outside, we found that the camp had been laid out in an orchard of fruit trees, almonds, and grape vines. What a setting compared with our previous abode.

That night we visited the Navy, Army and Air Force Institutes rooms, had tea and biscuits, and saw a film at the Hippodrome. The rest of the week we just relaxed and unwound, luxuriating in hot showers, good food and the cheerful company of those friendly Kiwis and Tommies. Each day on waking I had to pinch myself to make sure this was really happening, for on looking outside every morning, I fully expected to see lines of barbed wire and those tall sentry boxes, instead of which we looked out on a beautiful orchard.

The next two days we spent in camp, where we were paid 2000 lire (£5.00), a huge fistful of small grey notes, our first army pay in over three years. We were also given leave passes and told we were at liberty to go where we pleased. Bill and I wrote our first letters home as free men, the first in over three years, and I guessed our folks back home would get the surprise of their lives on learning that we were back behind our lines.

We took ourselves into Bari in the following days, enjoying the company of the Kiwis at their club. We also visited an officers' clothing shop, where we bought ourselves a good old Aussie hat and a rising sun badge; and the Bari aerodrome, where we went for a spin in a DC3 piloted by an Aussie from Bondi, a great bloke who had been over here for four years and expected to be a while yet on his tour of duty.

We circled Bari, then the pilot flew us over the harbour. Pointing down, he picked out the wrecks of the boats that had sunk when an ammunition ship blew up in the port about a week earlier.

'Boy,' he said, 'what a hell of a bang! We thought the Germans had got through our fighter defence and were bombing the harbour, and for a while all was bloody confusion until we found out what had actually happened.'

When we got back to camp that night our leave was cancelled, and we were told to get our packs ready and be prepared to move out the following morning. We were going to Naples.

10
By the Way We Came

Well, you know the old saying, 'See Naples and die,' and I guess that is what a lot of our brave soldiers did. Sadly, they never had a chance to admire the beauties of this grand old city, as they were otherwise engaged in the savage and bloody battles that raged in and around this historic place.

As we wandered amidst the shambles left in the aftermath of this terrible conflict, it was brought home to us how badly the poor civilian population had suffered. We were surrounded by dozens of people of all ages, and by their gaunt looks and half-starved appearance, you knew what they had undergone during the past few years. As they held out their hands for money or food, you had no doubt that their needs were genuine and truly desperate. We gave them what we could and left them there in those sordid surroundings, with 'grazie' and 'multo grazie' (thanks, many thanks) ringing in our ears. We felt humbled in the presence of such poverty and despair.

The following day a group of us went out to visit Pompeii. I always have a strange feeling of awe when I think of the mystery and wonder of those bygone ages, and as we walked down those narrow cobblestones streets, with ruts in them carved by Roman chariots, I tried to visualise the people and scenes of that great nation.

Our Italian guide, whom we christened Antonio, was a typical showman who elaborated with chuckles and flourishes as he pointed out the different items of interest. When he came to what he said was a Roman brothel, he pointed to the carvings on the stones outside, and sure enough we could see a man's penis pointing to the doorway.

Now I don't know whether some Italian artist had got to work on those stones or not, for the tourists' sake, but the likeness was for real. Anyway, we all trooped in wondering what to expect next, but it was just a plain stone-walled room, about 12 feet by 12. What took our eye, however, was a piece of coloured material draped over what looked like a picture hanging on the wall.

'What's under that, Antonio?' asked one of the hardened veterans in our group.

'Me make plenty money showing tourists before war,' says Antonio.

'We're His Majesty's bloody tourists, now give us a look,' said one of the boys.

'Tourists pay good money to see picture,' says Antonio. We got the message. By this time he had us well and truly hooked, and our curiosity aroused, we made a hurried collection and gave him a handful of lire.

'It had better be good, Antonio, or we'll knock your bloody block off.'

'Great masterpiece by unknown artist. Magnifico,' says Antonio, and with a sweeping flourish which reminded me of a Spanish bullfighter side-stepping the charge of a wild bull, Antonio whipped away the cloth.

The painting before us was about 18 inches by 18, and depicted a giant Roman centurion covered in armour, except for his huge penis, which judging by the soldier's height, must have been at least 12 inches long. There was more: the centurion was weighing his member on some scales. I would have thought the size alone would have satisfied him.

Well, there was uproar from the boys and some pretty lurid remarks, and a certain amount of envy. Some of the boys wanted to buy the painting, but there was no moving Antonio. He flatly refused, saying he could make much more money from the tourists than we could ever give him. So we all trooped out; quite a few bemoaned the fact they did not have a camera.

*   *   *

The next day we left Naples for Taranto on the same railway line on which, years before, I had gone north to an unknown destination. Now I found myself travelling south under very changed circumstances. What a difference in the state of mind and well-being between a prisoner under guard going north, and a free man going south.

We travelled most of that night down the west coast, looking out on the beautiful scenery of shoreline and sea, made more enchanting by bright moonlight. In Taranto we stayed in a transit camp for two days. What memories this place recalled for me. Two years ago I was here in an underground shelter whilst the harbour was being bombed by our Air Force. Now I could wander round without guards, and at night sit in a cinema and see a film called *Broadway Rhythm*, which we viewed in comfort without the sound of falling bombs.

We left Taranto on board the 15 000-ton *Dunbar Castle*, preceded by another boat of similar size carrying 2000 German soldiers to POW camps in either India or Egypt (or so I was told by one of our crew). What a reversal of fortune! A long time ago, I was escorted to a POW camp at Castelvetrano in Sicily, with bewilderment and despair in my heart, not knowing what lay ahead. So in a way, I knew exactly the trauma and feelings of those German soldiers on the boat ploughing ahead of us through the waves.

What an amazing lot of men were on board our ship: 17 nationalities, amongst them some Aussies from the RAF Bomber Command, who had been over here for about two years; English RAF personnel bound for the Far Eastern theatre of war; South African blacks; Palestinians; and a big crowd of 800 Kiwis who had just come out of the line in Italy and were going home to be demobbed after nearly four years overseas service — a better lot of blokes you would not find in a long day's march.

There were also some soldiers from the Polish Brigade, who were going on leave, and some sick and wounded on their way to base in Egypt. These Poles had had more moves than men on a chess board, for after they were captured by the Russians, they were sent to internment camps in Siberia to work in the forests cutting timber. When Britain signed an agreement with Stalin, however, they were allowed to return to the Allied lines. They made their way down to the Middle East through Iran and Iraq, finally ending up in Egypt, where they fought very bravely alongside our own men. They were now part of the Allied armies fighting their way up the Italian Peninsula. These poor men had not seen their families in over five years and did not know whether their womenfolk and children were dead or alive. What tragedy the Polish nation has suffered in two world wars and in the years since.

October 2. As the coast of Africa came into view dead ahead, the ship swung to port. For the next two days we steamed past that stretch of country where the tide of battle had swung back and forth for over two years, culminating in the bloody battle of El Alamein, where Rommel's force, the Panzerarmee Afrika, was defeated by the Allied army under Montgomery's command. Here my own battalion, the 2nd/13th of the Australian 9th Division, had fought to a standstill; almost half the men were either killed or seriously wounded during the savage fighting of the ten days of the final battle.

Here, men of opposing forces had fought with equal bravery, not so much for possession of the vast tracts of desert sweeping from horizon to horizon, but for their ideals, which they thought were right in their own eyes. The sad part about this terrible conflict was that the majority of men on both sides were brought up to be Christians. What a lasting impression it made on my mind to see, for the first time, in the camp at

Tripoli, the inscription on the German soldiers' belt buckles: 'Gott mit uns' (God with us).

October 4. Early in the morning we were all lining the rails, on deck to watch the sun rise out of the desert behind Alexandria. A blimp hovered over the harbour and minaret towers were poking through the early morning mists. What an inspiring sight!

We docked about 8:30 a.m. but had to remain on board to await transport. As I leant on the rail, gazing out over the city, I wondered what had happened to my kitbag, left behind in Alex' three years before when our convoy, 100 miles long, passed by on the desert road heading west to an unknown fate.

At two o'clock, we disembarked and boarded a train for Madi Camp, just outside Cairo, where we arrived at 11:15 p.m. We were then taken by truck to the 23rd Kiwi Ambulance lines, arriving there at midnight. The sergeants had a great meal dished up for us in their mess, and after it we were shown to our sleeping quarters in spotlessly clean huts and bedded down for the night on stretchers, between beautiful white sheets. What heaven! The hospitality of those Kiwis and their genuine warmth boosted the spirit of friendship we already felt for each other as a legacy of the comradeship of Gallipoli.

*　　　*　　　*

Cairo in '44, when the theatre of war had moved on, was an active, bustling and far more prosperous city than it had been before hostilities began. During the war, thousands of troops passed through or spent their leave in the city, and many were still there — some convalescing in hospital, some passing through on their way to the Far East theatre of war, while others, like ourselves and the Kiwis, were on their way home.

Cairo was a city that had just shed its years of darkness, and the sight as we approached it from Alexandria the previous night, was something to behold — the whole city was a blaze of lights, a spectacle we had not seen in four years.

On our first morning in this fascinating city we went to the pay office, where a Lieutenant Gorman paid us £30 sterling each. From then on, we seemed to be spending money like water, not that Bill and I had all that much to spend, but everything is relative. When you've had nothing for years, any money you do get seems to have considerably more value than its actual worth.

With a few Kiwis acting as our guides, Bill and I went slumming round the various bars, favourite haunts of the troops on leave. To mention just a few, there were the Spitfire, the African, the Royal, the Long, the

Mannering, and last but not least the Winter Bar, a joint owned by a Russian Jewish woman who had escaped from Russia to Shanghai after World War I, eventually making her way to Cairo, where she had resided for the last ten years. I guess she was quite well-off, with all those troops leaning on her bar, quenching their never-ending thirst. What a fascinating personality — flashing eyes, large earrings, a dazzling smile, and a constant patter in the jargon of the Middle East or the lingo of the troops lining her bar.

That night, more drunk than sober, we crawled into a gharry, the equivalent of an English barouche, a four-wheeled, horse-drawn carriage with a seat in front for the driver and seats inside for two couples facing each other. The hood was generally thrown back for sightseeing unless, of course, the passengers were to avail themselves of ladies of the night (as some soldiers used to do), and make their pleasure on the back seat. All this time the gharry driver would be cracking his whip and using language that would make your hair curl, language that was, I'm sure, a legacy of our boys of the Light Horse in the First World War, and helped along during the Second.

The next afternoon we were taken on a grand tour of Cairo by one of the finest men it has been my pleasure to meet, the famous and distinguished World War I photographer, Captain Frank Hurley. He took a crowd of us sightseeing, and what he did not know about all the byways and ancient mosques of Cairo was not worth knowing. Having been the official war photographer with our Light Horse, and being able to speak Arabic quite fluently, he gained entry to many places which otherwise we would not have had a hope of seeing.

*   *   *

For most people, I think, the memories that come flooding back to mind are those of the more pleasant kind. To me the ones that stand out are those associated with people, as against places, but when you get a combination of both, it's an experience of a lifetime. In wartime, too, everything seems to be tinged with a certain amount of unreality and excitement — people thrown together in different parts of the globe, who but for the war would never have met.

The people: the WAAFs; the place: the houseboat *Arabia*, tied up at a wharf on the banks of the Nile, the whole scene lit by bright moonlight shimmering on the waters of this historic river.

In the days before and just after the war, those who could afford it travelled to foreign parts in stately P&O liners, at a peaceful and leisurely pace and enjoying every minute of their voyage. These days people jet to far-flung places and think nothing of it, and characters like Molly Meldrum would most likely say, 'Cairo, what's so special about that? It's old hat, just like the one I've got on the top of my head.'

But this was Cairo in '44, and Bill and I did have a certain feeling of excitement as we were welcomed on board the well-lit pleasure craft by the wonderful WAAF girls who had organised a dance for us POWs and other members of the forces. For Bill and me, it was our first dance in four years.

The *Arabia* pulled away from the wharf into mid-stream and started up the Nile. Bill, with a twinkle in his eye, said, 'Now Basil, don't get carried away with these lovely looking girls.'

'Any one of these girls can carry me away with pleasure,' I said.

When the band started playing we were a bit shy, but of course the girls soon fixed that situation. They came forward and pulled us on to the dance floor, and soon we were swirling around with girls of many nationalities — Scottish, Czech, English, French, refugees from Austria, and last but not least Jewish refugees who had fled from the terrors of Hitler's Third Reich.

I found myself in the arms of one of these lovely Jewish girls, and half-way through the night we slipped away aft and made love under the stars, with the sound of band music wafting back along the deck, as they played the popular fox trots and quick steps of those times. But we were oblivious to our surroundings, soothed by the beautiful night and the gloriously soft moonlight shimmering on the waters of the Nile, with the lights of one of the most exotic cities in the world twinkling away in the distance.

The next afternoon, feeling somewhat washed out after the previous night's entertainment, Bill and I decided to pay a visit to that holy of holies, the one and only officers' retreat, Shepheards Hotel. We purchased a warrant officer's badge, hoping it would be sufficient to pass through the portals of this sacred shrine, and proceeded along one of those typically crowded streets, surrounded by bustling humanity, with the sound of cracking whips and the yells and curses of the noisy gharry drivers ringing in our ears.

Suddenly a small Arab boy appeared alongside Bill; I would say he was no more than 10 or 12 years old. He touched Bill on the arm, and holding up what appeared to be a gold-plated pen, he said, 'You buy pen, real gold pen, please mister.'

Bill took the pen, at the same time saying, 'I'll bet it's a bloody fraud, you little bugger,' and stopping in our tracks, we examined the pen. To our surprise, it looked the genuine article, with '18ct Gold. Made in England' stamped on it. Bill unscrewed the top, to see if it had a rubber tube inside, which it did, and after some haggling, Bill bought it at a bargain price.

But the little boy still continued to trot alongside us, and holding up a bottle of ink, said, 'Me fill pen for you please mister?' Bill thanked him and handed over the pen, whereupon the little merchant took to his heels and scampered down a side alley, hotly pursued by a cursing Bill, but of course the little rogue knew Cairo like the palm of his hand and very quickly disappeared in the crowd, leaving Bill swearing and fuming in frustration. So there and then we decided to down a couple of stiff whiskies, if and when we passed through the doors of the famous Shepheards.

We threaded out way down through the narrow streets of the brothel area, and eventually climbed the steps and went through the front entrance of the hotel, a huge monolith built in the early colonial days of the British Empire and like the pyramids a symbol of power.

Shepheards had been a meeting place for heads of the British Armed Forces in World War I, and also for the Allied forces in the Middle East during this Second World War, and as Bill and I had heard it, it was an officers-only hotel. But as we made our way through the very crowded foyer, we noted many nationalities: Arabs from the vastly rich oil regions of the Persian Gulf, well-dressed men from Europe and America, obviously here on business of one kind or another, a sprinkling of young women, and a few officers — from lieutenants upwards in rank to brigadiers and colonels, and downwards to insignificant warrant officers!

The foyer itself had the antique look about it of a bygone era — huge round pillars going up to a very high ceiling, potted palms in the corners, and I would not have been surprised had there been aspidistras in place of the palms. The pillars and walls were painted in browns and greens, with touches of red and blue added to the colour scheme, and as we walked through to the lounge, we passed two bronze women holding up lamps.

The lounge was crowded and noisy, with the smoke of many cigarettes making a hazy atmosphere, and both bars were packed. There was a small bar at the entrance, but we chose the large bar at the far end of the lounge, and strolled nonchalantly down to get our whiskies.

Standing to one side, we took stock of our surroundings, which were truly amazing. The decor was Edwardian or Victorian, with large stained-glass windows and leather-covered divans. Through one of the many arches we could see the garden bar and a dance floor in a wonderful setting amongst trees festooned with lights. Over in one corner a young lieutenant was seated at a piano playing one of Chopin's beautiful melodies.

I looked around at all these groups engaged in animated and lively conversation, and I could picture the scene as it was before the First World War and between the two wars: the elegant women, the dashing officers, the latest music and dances. Now here we were again in the throes of another world war, with this old lounge full to overflowing, people sitting on the divans talking about their hopes, their loved ones, the progress of the war on the various battle fronts, and all things pertaining to the past, present and future. I wondered what lay ahead.

I was awakened from my reverie as Bill gave me a nudge and said, 'Come on Basil, down your whisky and let's have a look round the hotel, then get cracking before some bloke with real tabs on his shoulders asks us some awkward questions.'

We wandered through this huge place and were astonished at the number of convenient services under the one roof. There were banks, a post office, large reading rooms with comfortable lounges, and a big dining room packed with people of every nationality. We pitied the poor waiters taking all those multi-lingual orders.

Having satisfied our curiosity, Bill and I strolled out through the main entrance. Little did we realise that within a few years King Farouk's reign would come to a violent end, his place would be taken by Muhammad Naguib, the new premier of Egypt, and Britain's rule would come to an end. During the turbulent period of King Farouk's overthrow, the mobs took to the streets with flaming torches, and this grand old hotel, once the symbol of British authority in the Middle East, was burnt to the ground.

11
Across the Oceans

On Sunday, October 15th, we boarded the Orient Line ship *Orontes* at Port Taufiq. Boy, what a shemozzle! On board were nearly 5000 troops, and the first thing we heard from some of the men, in no uncertain manner, was that she was bloody well overcrowded, and that at the beginning of the voyage there had nearly been a riot. Fortunately, after Bill and I boarded her, the food improved, which was just as well, as the boys were fairly stirred up about it and there had been some ugly scenes.

Bill and I were lucky enough to be on B deck, but we still felt the terrific heat. When we went down to our meals on the mess deck — at 7 a.m., 12 noon and 6 at night — it was as though we were going into a sauna bath, and the meal over, there was an unholy rush for the top deck.

We had on board some 2000 RAF airmen, naval personnel and British troops, all bound for India, also 300 Aussies, and as we made our way down the Gulf of Suez and into the Red Sea, the conditions were such that it seemed — like scones — we were slowly being cooked in a mobile oven. At night, hundreds of men were to be seen carrying a single blanket as they scrambled up from below to get a position on A deck, where they spent the whole night trying to get some sleep.

Four days later we arrived at Aden, where the British operated both a naval base and an air force base covering the whole of the region and points beyond. As we approached the entrance to the harbour, Bill and I were joined by a British officer, who told us that he had been in Aden just before the war. He knew the history of the place like the palm of his hand, and leaning on the rail, he pointed out the various places of interest and told us all about this fascinating outpost, which we had vaguely read about in our geography lessons at school.

He told us that in summer it was reputed to be the hottest place on earth, and for British personnel it was mercifully only an 18 months' station. He went on to say that Aden had been under British rule since

129

1839. He pointed out the two peninsulas which form the harbour (Aden and little Aden); they are volcanic rock, roughly oval in shape and connected to the low sandy shore by short stretches of land. Crater Town, as it was known, had a fairly large population of Arabs (who formed the majority), and there were also Indians, Jews, Somalis, Europeans and other nationalities — in all a total of approximately 80 000, including military personnel.

The officer, John Shrewsbury, was a splendid historian and better than any tourist guide. He told us about the ancient water tanks, of pre-Islamic origin, and how the British had repaired them in the middle of the 19th century by damming the Wadi Tewela at the upper end of the town. With careful management, the 13 tanks could hold upwards of 80 million gallons of water, and had been the town's main water supply since the last century. Alas we were unable to see them, as we were not given shore leave.

As we moved up the harbour, we could see church and mosque spires rising above the white-washed, mud-brick houses, all laid out in military style. There were also army, navy and air force barracks, as Britain had quite a large permanent force stationed there.

During the day, hardly anyone moved out of doors, but at dusk the town came to life. Europeans, dressed mainly in white, could be seen strolling along the foreshore, and as there was no blackout, it was a wonderful sight once again to see the lights come on. At intervals along both sides of the main road beautiful blue mercury lights were gleaming in the darkness, casting a soft, gentle glow on the roofs of this remote outpost.

As darkness fell, what a spectacular sight to see the lights of the warships and troopships come on one after the other, while from the *Orion,* anchored nearby, the sound of singing came drifting across the bay, the soldiers giving 'There'll Always be an England' a throaty rendition. I guess the heroic defence of the British Isles over the last four years had somewhat proved the words of that stirring song.

At seven o'clock the following morning, those of us who were not at the first sitting for mess were up on deck to watch as the anchors of most of the ships in the harbour were weighed. The warships led the way out through the minefields, followed by the troopships. What a stirring sight to see our convoy fall into line ahead, with destroyers screening us way out to starboard and port. The convoy consisted of the *Orontes, Orion, Warwick Castle, Rhangi* and a couple of Liberty ships, and as we headed out into the early morning heat of the Arabian Sea, I turned to take one last look at this small but significant outpost of Empire, knowing that I would probably never see it again.

We sweated our way slowly across the Arabian Sea, which was quite calm. We assumed that the speed of our convoy was governed not only by the slowest ship, but by the constant changes in direction (evasive action) we needed to make in case we ran into submarines (a definite possibility, hence the screen of destroyers). But our voyage was quite uneventful, and five days later we dropped anchor in Bombay Harbour, where almost four years earlier, to the day, our battalion had disembarked from the *Queen Mary* and entrained for the British Army rest camp at Deolali, about 100 miles from Bombay.

Leaning on the rail before leaving the ship, we gazed out over this city of teeming millions, then known as the gateway to British India and made famous by that nostalgic old marching song:

> *A troopship was leaving Bombay,*
> *Bound for old Blighty's shore,*
> *Heavily laden with time expired men,*
> *Bound for the land they adore. (Origin unknown.)*

Suddenly we heard our names being called, and on looking down at the wharf, we could hardly believe our eyes, for standing there like apparitions were some of the boys we'd left behind in the main camp, Stalag 344 at Lamsdorf. When Bill and I disembarked, we greeted one another like long-lost friends, as I suppose we were. I don't know who was the most surprised; we had said our good-byes back in Germany, but the difference was that while Bill and I were reasonably healthy, they were sick men and were being repatriated home, through the auspices of the International Red Cross, in exchange for German POWs in the same condition.

Our greetings over, we were told to climb into some trucks. We were driven to a British Army rest camp on the other side of the bay and allocated beds in long huts, which had big ceiling fans cooling us down day and night, though at this time of the year the evenings were beginning to cool down. The camp was in a beautiful location amongst tall trees, and at night the scent of frangipani wafted in through the windows, adding another touch of the exotic to this strange and wonderful country.

The next morning, while wandering round camp and familiarising ourselves with our surroundings, we met some British troops who were on leave from the Burma front. What a sorry sight they were — pale and sickly yellow from taking Mepacrine over a long period to combat the effects of the deadly malaria fever, which is carried by the anopheles mosquito. These blokes didn't say much, but judging by the look of the poor blighters, we guessed it must have been hell out there in that God-forsaken jungle, especially during the monsoon season, when they would be up to their knees in mud and slush and suffering from heat, high humidity, and tropical diseases.

*   *   *

The notorious and infamous Grant Road of Bombay! The commanding officer placed it out of bounds to the troops in our camp, and that, of course, was an added incentive to Bill and me and a couple of the Kiwis to hire a gharry that night after mess and proceed forthwith to see the sights of this road of ill-repute.

We told the driver to slow down as we entered Grant Road. The sight was mind-boggling. Down one side we saw what appeared to be row on row of cages. Half of each room was partitioned off and there was straw on the floor. Standing behind the bars, selling their bodies, were women of all shapes and sizes, some just young girls in their teens. On passing one of these cages, we had another eye-opener. We saw a huge man standing on the footpath with his arm through the bars, fondling the breasts of one of these poor unfortunate girls, who, I was told, would be paid only the equivalent of one shilling for her service, whilst for those upstairs in the dress circle, so to speak, the charge was slightly higher, two or three shillings.

What degradation for these poor unfortunate women, who were forced through circumstances of poverty, in this city of teeming millions, to eke out a meagre existence in these sordid surroundings.

By contrast, the following day, we decided to visit a high-class brothel in one of the better suburbs, a big two-storey house set in very beautiful gardens, with trees and shrubs dotting the well-kept landscape.

The door was opened by a rather striking Indian woman of middle age, dressed in a beautiful sari, who greeted us with: 'Good day gentlemen, please come in,' and thereupon ushered us into a large oblong room. Scattered round the polished floors were glorious Indian rugs; beautiful paintings adorned the walls; and arranged on either side of the room were rows of quite luxurious armchairs. Then bidding us goodbye in that pleasant lisping voice so characteristic of the people of that strange and fascinating land, our hostess left the room.

Taking our seats, the six of us did not have to wait long before a bevy of girls made their entrance and paraded round the room. Some of the boys paired up and disappeared, but Bill and I were not very taken with their looks and made some casual remarks about keeping them at arm's length, let alone the shorter distance that the girls expected. Of course the girls understood our remarks only too well. Scowling at us, they told us in no uncertain terms what to do with our money, and stamped out of the room. It was a good entertaining half hour.

The next day I went into a large retail store to purchase a few gifts to take home to the folks. Behind the counter was an attractive Indian girl. I told her I was an Australian and also mentioned how well she spoke English. I was rather taken aback by her quick, somewhat sharp reply, 'Why shouldn't I, the British own our country, don't they?'

Well, I was taken by surprise and at a loss for a suitable reply, knowing full well that what she said was perfectly true, so paying for my goods, I left the shop. I had not gone more than a hundred yards down the street when I heard footsteps behind me and a girl's voice call out 'Please sir,' and turning round, I was surprised to see the girl from behind the counter.

'I wish to apologise for my rudeness,' she said. 'You are not British, but Australian.' I told her she should not have worried, and after some small talk she asked Bill and me to a dance that night, giving me directions on how to get to the dance hall, and after telling me her name, she hurried back to the shop.

Walking back to camp, I though about what that lovely girl had said to me in the shop, the meaning of her words so clear: freedom. She was speaking not only for herself, but for the whole of India, and as future events have turned out, Britain, abiding by the United Nations Charter to the letter, has lowered her flag on many poles, in many lands, and her once vast empire, like the Roman, has gone into the limbo of the past, and on those same poles now fly the flags of independent nations, whose people can raise their heads with pride to see that symbol of freedom fluttering in the breeze.

When I got back to camp, I found that all personnel going to Australia and beyond were confined to barracks; no leave would be granted that night. I was rather disappointed about the dance and often wonder what the very attractive girl must have thought about me — whether I had snubbed her for her remarks. I sincerely hope she found out that we had shipped home.

The next day we were at sea on the Liberty ship USS *General A.E. Anderson*, averaging 20 to 21 knots, or approximately 500 miles in 24 hours. The trip grew fairly monotonous; our only visitors were the occasional sea birds and flying fish skimming the deep blue waters of the Indian Ocean. Ship's inspection and boat drill took place every morning at ten thirty, after which we were free to do what we pleased. On this part of the voyage home we were unescorted, presumably because of our speed and because we were so far from the actual war zone that the prospect of attack from enemy submarines or warships was much less. No one worried about the absence of the usual destroyers.

Some of our boys lounged around the deck reading books, or else took themselves down below to one of the holds, where, through a thick haze of smoke, one could make out the poker games from the masklike faces of the players, or watch the large group of men gathered in a circle playing 'two-up,' commonly known as 'swi' in good old Aussie lingo. On the floor in front of each player were large piles of money or big stacks of cartons of American cigarettes, which back home in Australia could be exchanged for almost anything, including, so rumour had it, ladies' favours.

Being an American ship, the food was very good and plentiful, but generally rich with a lot of sweets, and of course Bill and I, not being used to such fare, got stuck into it with a gusto. Our stomachs suffered accordingly, and a visit to the medical officer was the order of each day.

We made our way down towards the Southern Ocean and round into the Great Australian Bight. At long last we were on the final leg for home. Up till now the voyage had been quite uneventful.

There were some bad malaria cases on board, also some troppo cases from the Burma front, and we heard that one of these poor blokes had jumped overboard on the first night out of Bombay and was never recovered, but as the story was latrine rumour, I was never able to verify its authenticity.

On a beautiful sunny day not long after we entered the Bight, I was lying on the deck reading, when all of a sudden, over the ship's PA system came the cry 'Man overboard aft,' which was repeated several times, and looking up at the crow's-nest, we saw the man on duty pointing and shouting out directions. We all rushed to the rail, and sure enough we could see a head bobbing in the waves and fast disappearing in the distance. The ship gradually lost way, and turning in a wide circle, retraced its course, but although nearly everyone on board was keeping a sharp lookout, we failed to locate the unfortunate soldier who, we were told, had overbalanced as he was leaning over the rail being seasick. According to one eyewitness, a chap standing near him had made a frantic effort to save him. He had even managed to get hold of one leg, but could not hang on because the weight was too much, and the man was wrenched from his grasp. What a sad end for a soldier on his way home.

Two days later I was lounging on the deck, when once again, darn me if we did not have a repeat performance. 'Man overboard aft,' came the voice over the PA, and as before we all rushed to the rail. Sure enough another head was bobbing in the waves, and sailing outwards towards the man in the water was a lifebuoy, flung by one of the crew. There was a lot of shouting and yelling, and the ship's officers were giving orders to man the lifeboat and get it ready for lowering while the ship put about, which took some time as we were travelling at about 20 knots.

Once we had retraced our course, the man in the crow's-nest shouted and pointed, but try as we may, we could not see anything, and although the boat was lowered and the men rowed furiously in the direction the lookout indicated, there was no sign of the missing soldier. As darkness was almost upon us, the boat returned and was hastily pulled up on board the ship, which immediately gathered speed and raced away out of the area in case a lone enemy submarine was lurking in the depths below.

A tall laconic Texan standing on the deck alongside me let out a sharp rebuke. 'What's wrong with these bastards?' he drawled. 'I was on a British troopship in the Atlantic and we had a man go overboard, but he was rescued in half an hour, while these blokes lose two men in a matter of a few days.' And with that he stamped off and went below, probably to vent his anger on the poker or swi games.

The last man lost overboard was a troppo case who wanted to go to the toilet but eluded his guard, raced up on deck, and jumped overboard. To this day I can still see those heads bobbing in the blue waters of the Bight, gradually disappearing into the distance.

We were nearing the end of the voyage. Excitement was running high. We were all caught up with a fever of expectation and a couple of shrewd cookies ran a raffle, the aim of which was to guess the hour and minute when the first rope from the ship was tied up at the wharf. Well, I reckon those two blokes must have been psychologists, because boy, when the ship berthed, Bill and I and hundreds of others would be leaning over the rail, all thoughts of raffle completely forgotten as we looked down on the sea of faces and waving arms below, each of us searching for our loved ones, whilst who knows, the raffle kings were chuckling to themselves.

At long last, on the morning of November 17th, 1944, we made our way slowly up Port Phillip Bay, and through the heat haze we could make out the distant shoreline and the tops of the high-rise buildings clustered round the northern end of the bay.

Bill and I were leaning on the rail as we finally tied up to the wharf at Princes Pier, and I guess we both had lumps in our throats as we gazed down on that sea of upturned faces and waving handkerchiefs while a brass band played that grand old tune 'Waltzing Matilda' to welcome us home after four long years away from this land so dear to our hearts.

Suddenly Bill nudged me, and pointing down, he said, 'There's my brother Jack and my two sisters,' and looking at this tough and very staunch friend, I could detect a certain amount of moisture in his eyes and guessed how he felt after those long years of separation.

We disembarked and Bill's two sisters rushed forward to embrace and kiss him, while his brother shook him warmly by the hand and gave him a big hug. I could see they were a very close knit family. I stood by quietly and watched this emotional scene, and knew that Bill had made it home for Xmas.

When all the excitement of the family reunion had died down somewhat, Bill turned and introduced me, saying quietly, 'This is my mate Basil, who has been with me through all our travels, and if I may say so, he's a great bloke.' Of course it was my turn to be hugged and kissed by the two sisters and receive a firm handshake from Bill's older brother Jack. We were whisked away to transit camp, but not before making some arrangements to have dinner at the Menzies Hotel with Bill's family that night.

Well, we were certainly given the VIP treatment that evening, and it was many years since Bill and I had sat down to such a wonderful meal. I think Jack had tipped off the staff, as the service was excellent. First came oyster mornay, which was followed by a large rump steak with all the trimmings, and topped off with blackberry pie and cream.

'A slight improvement on your POW tucker,' said Jack with a grin as he filled our glasses with a deliciously smooth red wine. Then he got to his feet to make a short speech, saying how wonderful it was to have us back home once again safe and sound, but that he and his sisters were taken by surprise, as we had arrived somewhat earlier than they had expected. With this remark, which sent us all into fits of laughter, he sat down.

So passed a glorious evening, one of those one does not forget in a hurry, and by its end we were all somewhat tiddly, but who cared if we made the hotel ring with raucous laughter as Bill and I recalled some of the more humorous anecdotes of our POW life. Finally that wonderful evening came to an end, and thanking Jack and his sisters for that sumptuous meal, we said our good-byes, and in the early hours, Bill and I staggered back to camp.

The next morning we were paid and I was given a rail ticket to my home state. Bill would be going home with his brother Jack to Orbost, Victoria, when he was given leave.

Midday found Bill and me standing on the platform at Flinders Street Station. Our talk was of the desultory kind. We did not say much — we had no need to, for as our hands clasped in farewell, we knew that the spirit of comradeship forged in POW camps and during the three months of our escape would last for the rest of our lives. At one o'clock, with a hissing and a puffing from the mighty, powerful steam engine up front, we slowly pulled out of the station, and leaning out of the window, I yelled out, 'See you soon, old mate'.

'Maybe for Xmas, Basil,' he shouted back, with a grin, and we both laughed.

The great old engine roared through the night, and I for one could hardly sleep, what with my excitement and the anticipation of seeing my folks once again. The clicketty-clack of the wheels and the shrill warning blasts from the engine as it approached the crossings also made it rather difficult to sleep. We changed trains at the border, and at dawn I found myself standing in the corridor looking out the window as the old familiar landscape gradually came to life in the early morning sunrise, as we rushed away northwards.

The countryside here was also brown and bare, burnt by the fierce heat of a drought. The long hot dry spell had made its mark, and the paddocks were all scorched, with no sign of green except for the occasional patch of irrigation on some of the properties lucky enough to have rivers running through them or dams from which to pump water.

At last this longest journey of my life was coming to a close. As we raced through Strathfield and the inner suburbs of Sydney, and when Redfern flashed by, I knew we were near to journey's end. Finally, with a hissing of steam and the gradual grinding of the wheels on the tracks, we pulled into the platform at Central Station.

I guess I was a bit nervous about getting off that train, wondering if my parents were there to meet me, although I was told they had been notified of my arrival in Sydney. I was also wondering how kindly or otherwise the war had affected their general health. Well, I stepped down on to the platform and made my way slowly towards the entrance, and sure enough they were both standing there, my mother pointing excitedly in my direction, and my old dad waving. I rushed forward and threw my arms around them and was smothered by my mother's kisses and the warm, friendly hug of my dad, and at long last I knew I had come home for Xmas.

Postcript

Bill Irvine returned to his farm at Orbost Victoria and died some years ago.

I never saw or heard of *Scotty* after our last meeting in Banská Bystrica. Nothing is known of *Gordon Fallis* after he and Scotty separated. He may have joined the partisans and may have died with them. After the war I wrote to his home address in New Zealand, but never received a reply.

APPENDIX
The Slovakian Uprising

Below is a bare-bones description of events leading up to the Slovakian Uprising of 1944 that I hope will provide a context for Chapters 7 and 8. In researching the topic, I consulted half a dozen sources. These varied considerably in their analysis of the events, especially in regards to the role of President Benes, the communist partisans and the USSR. One writer, for instance, suggests that the USSR orchestrated the uprising (which was doomed to failure from the start) as a way of sowing disorder, thus paving the way for an eventual takeover by the Red Army. Given the history of the region in the intervening years, this view is hardly surprising.

*   *   *

Czechoslovakia had ceased to exist as a country even before the war began. It lost the Sudetenland to Germany as a result of the Munich Agreement of September 1938, then in March 1939 the Reich swallowed up Bohemia and Moravia, the Czech half of the country. Slovakia also lost a large slice of its territory (mostly) to Hungary; what remained became a Nazi puppet state under Monsignor Jozef Tiso.

Edvard Beneš, President of the Czech Republic, was forced to resign in October 1938. He and other exiles organised a Czechoslovak government-in-exile in London and worked for an Allied renunciation of the Munich Agreement, which they achieved in 1942. Beneš also worked to maintain friendly relations with the Soviet Union, in part to avoid Soviet encouragement of a communist coup in Czechoslovakia after the war. Before leaving for Britain, he had helped to organise a resistance network both inside the country and abroad; the government-in-exile collaborated with it throughout the war.

Resistance within Slovakia covered a wide range of ideologies and was at first fragmented. There were major differences between factions over what should happen to Slovakia at the end of the war. Communist partisans looked naturally to Moscow, yet as Bill and Basil learned in their dealings with ordinary citizens, the bulk of the population wanted Slovakia to remain part of a free, democratic Czechoslovakia, though with a greater say than it had had before. It should be noted that a large part of the Slovak army was sympathetic to the partisans.

In his 1942 Christmas broadcast from London, Beneš called on resistance groups in Slovakia to work towards a coup. In the spring of '43 secret police liquidated the Communist Party organisation in Slovakia, but the party was able to re-form that July. In December 1943 communist and democratic resistance leaders agreed to form a Slovak National Council (SNR) that would act in concert with the government-in-exile. This agreement also provided for a close association with the Soviet Union in both foreign policy and military affairs.

Beneš endorsed the agreement in March 1944, and the chief of staff of the military command at Banksá Bystrica, Lt. Col. Ján Golian, was given the task of preparing the army coup against the Tiso government. At that time, the Allies were bogged down in Italy and had yet to land in France; their assistance could hardly be counted on. The uprising was thus planned in conjunction with the Soviet army, which by then had approached the country's eastern borders. The idea was that the two best-equipped Slovak divisions, stationed in eastern Slovakia, would open up the Carpathian passes for the Soviet army, while the rear of the army would safeguard the strategic centre of the uprising against any German retaliation. Banská Bystrica was to be the geographical centre of the action.

Arguing that he needed more troops to fight the Soviet threat, Golian managed to obtain a decree from the Tiso government mobilising additional age groups. He was also able to move army units to the area and obtain valuable military supplies, food and medicines. The Slovak Minister of Defence was aware to some extent of the preparations for the uprising, but neither the Tiso government nor its German 'advisers' had any idea what was going on.

About this time, however, there was a change in Soviet strategy. The USSR now proposed to approach the area from the south, but only in the final months of the war. The Military Centre in Banská Bystrica was not made aware of this. On August 25, pro-Soviet partisans, acting without the knowledge of the SNR or the London Czechs, precipitated action when they:

> ... intercepted a train ... in which the German military mission under General Paul von Otto was returning from Bucharest to Berlin ... On the following day all twenty-eight of the mission were shot by the partisans. The news of their killing outraged the Germans. On August 28 Ludin [the German minister in Bratislava] informed Tiso that Slovakia would be occupied on the following day. On August 29, at 7.15 p.m, General Catlos announced the news of the German occupation over Radio Bratislava and ordered the Slovak army not to resist the Germans. Three-quarters of an hour later the Military Center at Banská Bystrica telephoned a signal to garrisons all over Slovakia to resist the Germans. The first armed encounter with the Germans took place on the same day in the area of Zilina ...
>
> The uprising transformed Slovakia, which until its outbreak had been a

peaceful hinterland, into a battlefront. In response to a call to arms issued by the SNR, men from all over Slovakia streamed to Banská Bystrica, to take up the struggle for Slovak freedom and honor.*

But the partisans had acted too soon, and there were irreparable losses in the early days of the uprising. The Germans converged on Slovakia from several directions. Slovak garrisons in western Slovakia were surprised and disarmed almost without a struggle. By the middle of September the Germans had secured both western and eastern Slovakia, and the insurgent area became isolated from the Soviet army by a wide band of territory. [The Red Army, assisted by the I Czechoslovak (exile) Corps, suffered 80 000 casualties in their attempts to come to the aid of the uprising.]

But when the Germans assaulted the stronghold in central Slovakia, they encountered stiff resistance and were forced to halt, regroup their forces, and bring reinforcements from other fronts. Finally, with 40 000 men, tanks, heavy artillery and planes, they overwhelmed the insurgent army. Banská Bystrica fell on October 27. Survivors melted into the Tatra Mountains and local partisan fighting continued until the liberation.

The uprising posed a grave problem for Germany at a critical time. It tied down forces needed on other fronts, it deprived it of a safe corridor to eastern Europe, and there were grievous losses of life and materiel. At the end of the uprising there were brutal reprisals against both insurgents and the civilian population.

From its beginning until liberation, 7500 soldiers and 2500 partisans were killed and 3723 civilians—men, women, and children—were murdered and buried in mass graves; 900 were burned in lime kilns; 30 000 people were deported to German concentration camps; 60 communities were completely destroyed by fires and 142 were partially wiped out. (Josko, p. 383)

*   *   *

Bill and Basil escaped from Slovakia as the result of an extraordinary series of coincidences. If they had not stumbled on the village that very day, or arrived in Banská Bystrica when they did, they may well have perished at the hands of the Germans. Partisan forces included a number of escaped prisoners of war.

A mystery for me is the identify of the leader who interviewed Bill and Basil and farewelled them at the airfield. In Anna Josko's words, 'Golian ... remained the commander until the arrival of Gen. Rudolf Viest from London on October 7. Golian then became Viest's deputy.' Before the war, Viest had been the only Slovak general in the Czechoslovak army, but had fled to Britain in early 1939.

*   Josko, Anna. 1973. The Slovak Resistance Movement. in ed. Victor S. Mamatey and Radomír Luza, *A History of the Czechoslovak Republic 1918-1948*, Princeton University Press, Princeton, New Jersey, pp. 376-77.

This is purely speculation, but the fact that the leader spoke fluent English may suggest that the men met Viest rather than Golian. If so, this would imply a confusion of dates on Josko's part. None of my other sources give a date for Viest's arrival. Basil reports that the leader had been flown out from Britain, but this was anecdotal information obtained only later. Both Viest and Golian were executed by the Germans.

June Hall

Index

www.trigafilms.co.uk
www.scallyteens.co.uk
www gaydyduk.com
http://blito.escortwww.com
www.superscort.com